BBC Books, an imprint of Ebury Publishing
20 Vauxhall Bridge Road,
London SW1V 2SA

BBC Books is part of the Penguin Random House group of companies
whose addresses can be found at global.penguinrandomhouse.com

Penguin
Random House
UK

First published by BBC Books in 2021

www.penguin.co.uk

A CIP catalogue record for this book is available from the British Library

ISBN 9781785946363

Commissioning editor: Albert DePetrillo
Project editor: Daniel Sorensen
Production: Phil Spencer

Printed and bound in Great Britain by Clays Ltd., Elcograf S.p.A.

The authorised representative in the EEA is Penguin Random House
Ireland, Morrison Chambers, 32 Nassau Street, Dublin DO2 YH68

Penguin Random House is committed to a sustainable future for
our business, our readers and our planet. This book is made
from Forest Stewardship Council® certified paper.

MIX
Paper from
responsible sources
FSC
www.fsc.org
FSC® C018179

Match of the Day magazine is published by Immediate Media Company
London Limited under license from BBC Studios

WELCOME!

This is Match of the Day magazine's Footy Facts & Stats Book

LOADING...

THE ULTIMATE FOOTBALL SUPERBRAIN!

It's bursting with thousands – literally thousands – of brilliant facts and amazing stats from the world of football.

It contains EVERYTHING you need to know about the game's biggest legends, the most iconic moments and the greatest tournaments.

Dive into the amazing world of football's incredible record-breakers – we're talking big-money transfers, net-busting strikers, red-card collecting hardmen and more.

Oh, and you'll learn how to say 'football' in every language!

MY FACT FILE

My name
....

My age
....

My hometown
....

....

My favourite team
....

....

STICK A PHOTO OF YOURSELF HERE!

All stats correct up to 1 June 2021

MATCH OF THE DAY FOOTY FACTS & STATS BOOK

CONTENTS

CLUB FOOTBALL

In 1888, the very first Football League season kicked off in England. Preston North End went the whole campaign unbeaten, winning the league by 11 points, to beome the original Invincibles.

■ Club football has come a long way since those black-and-white days, both in England and around the world.

There are now more than 200 national leagues across the globe – from the Andorran Primera Divisio to the Zambian Super League – and each and every one brings fans drama, excitement and magical memories.

The English Premier League has some of the best teams and players in the world, and together with Spain's La Liga, Italy's Serie A, Germany's Bundesliga and Ligue 1 in France, they make up the big five.

Their matches are beamed into houses in every continent around the world, and shirts of their clubs are worn in cities, towns and villages all over the planet.

During the 2018-19 season, which was won by Man. City, the Premier League was shown in 188 of the world's 193 countries recognised by the United Nations!

The Bundesliga is the best-supported league in the world with a higher average attendance than any other country!

The world's two richest clubs both come from Spain's La Liga – they are, of course, Barcelona and Real Madrid!

ENGLAND

THE COUNTRY

Population 56 million **Area** 130,279 km²
Currency Pound sterling
Capital London (9 million)
Other major cities Manchester, Birmingham, Leeds

PREMIER LEAGUE

Full name Football Association Premier League
Founded 1992 (29 years ago)
Number of clubs 20
Domestic cups FA Cup, EFL Cup
Website premierleague.com

BIGGEST STADIUMS

1 Old Trafford Man. United, 74,140

2 Tottenham Hotspur Stadium Tottenham, 62,850	**3 Emirates Stadium** Arsenal 60,704

MOST PREMIER LEAGUE TITLES

1 Man. United	13
2= Chelsea	5
2= Man. City	5
4 Arsenal	3
5 Blackburn, Leicester & Liverpool	1

BEST PLAYER OF ALL TIME

THIERRY HENRY
ARSENAL, 1999-2007, 2012
Prolific French forward who terrorised defences. He won a record four Golden Boots, two Prem titles, was twice PFA Player of the Year and is Arsenal's record scorer – and he did it all with pace and grace!

MOST EXPENSIVE SIGNING

£89m

PAUL POGBA, Juventus to Man. United, 2016

MOST PREMIER LEAGUE APPEARANCES

1 GARETH BARRY
Aston Villa, Man. City, Everton, West Brom, 1998-2018 **653 games**

2 RYAN GIGGS
Man. United, 1992-2014 **632 games**

3 FRANK LAMPARD
West Ham, Chelsea, Man. City, 1996-2015 **609 games**

MOST PREMIER LEAGUE GOALS

3 ANDY COLE
Newcastle, Man. United, Blackburn, Fulham, Man. City, Portsmouth, Sunderland, 1993-2008 **187 goals**

1 ALAN SHEARER
Blackburn, Newcastle, 1992-2006 **260 goals**

2 WAYNE ROONEY
Everton, Man. United, 2002-18 **208 goals**

ENGLAND

PREMIER LEAGUE SUPERCLUB

MAN. UNITED

Founded 1878 **Stadium** Old Trafford **Capacity** 74,140 **Manager** Ole Gunnar Solskjaer
Most Prem games Ryan Giggs, 632 **Most Prem goals** Wayne Rooney, 183
Club icons George Best, Bobby Charlton, Ryan Giggs, Eric Cantona, Paul Scholes

PREMIER LEAGUE SUPERCLUB

LIVERPOOL

Founded 1892 **Stadium** Anfield **Capacity** 53,394 **Manager** Jurgen Klopp **Most Prem games** Jamie Carragher, 508 **Most Prem goals** Robbie Fowler, 128 **Club icons** Steven Gerrard, Kenny Dalglish, Ian Rush, Robbie Fowler, Jamie Carragher

PREMIER LEAGUE SUPERCLUB

MAN. CITY

Founded 1880 **Stadium** Etihad Stadium **Capacity** 55,017 **Manager** Pep Guardiola
Most Prem games David Silva, 281 **Most Prem goals** Sergio Aguero, 181
Club icons David Silva, Vincent Kompany, Colin Bell, Francis Lee, Sergio Aguero

PREMIER LEAGUE SUPERCLUB

CHELSEA

Founded 1905 **Stadium** Stamford Bridge
Capacity 40,834 **Head Coach** Thomas
Tuchel **Most Prem games** John Terry, 492
Most Prem goals Frank Lampard, 147
Club icons Frank Lampard, John Terry,
Gianfranco Zola, Didier Drogba, Eden Hazard

PREMIER LEAGUE SUPERCLUB

ARSENAL

Founded 1886 **Stadium** Emirates Stadium
Capacity 60,704 **Manager** Mikel Arteta
Most Prem games Ray Parlour, 333
Most Prem goals Thierry Henry, 175 **Club
icons** Thierry Henry, Dennis Bergkamp,
Ian Wright, Tony Adams, Patrick Vieira

ENGLAND

THE GREATEST OF ALL TIME?

This is Man. City's record-breaking title-winning team from the 2017-18 season. Pep Guardiola's side smashed a ton of records that campaign – with many calling them the best Premier League team ever!

106
Most goals in a season

100
Most points in a season

32
Most wins in a season

16
Most away wins in a season

19 points
Biggest title-winning margin

+79
Best goal difference in a season

THE SUPER SIX

Six clubs have been in the Premier League since it began and never been relegated...

☑ ARSENAL ☑ CHELSEA
☑ EVERTON ☑ LIVERPOOL
☑ MAN. UNITED
☑ TOTTENHAM

THE YO-YO CLUBS

West Brom and Norwich share the record of most Prem promotions and relegations – both clubs have been promoted and relegated **FIVE times!**

GLORY, GLORY, MAN. UNITED

It may be the blue half of Manchester that's winning most of the silverware these days, but Man. United can quite rightly claim to be the best Prem club of all time – here's why...

UNITED IN THE PREMIER LEAGUE ERA

■ Have won more titles than any club ■ Have won more games than any club ■ Have scored more goals than any club ■ Have collected more points than any club ■ Have the best goal difference of any club

PREMIER LEAGUE LEGENDS

RYAN GIGGS
Most titles **13** Most seasons played **22**
Most seasons scored **21** Most assists **162**

SIR ALEX FERGUSON
Most titles **13** Most matches won **528**
Most points **1,752** Most Manager of the Season **11** Most Manager of the Month **27**

DON'T FORGET THE INVINCIBLES

Only one Prem club has gone the whole season unbeaten. In 2003-04, Arsenal romped to the Prem title undefeated. They were unbeaten for 49 games between May 2003 and October 2004 – a Prem record!

DID YOU KNOW?

The longest unbeaten run in Premier League history belongs to Chelsea. The Blues went an incredible 86 home games without losing between February 2004 and October 2008!

PREMIER LEAGUE

TOP SCORING PLAYERS IN PREMIER LEAGUE HISTORY

PLAYER	GOALS	GAMES	YEARS
1 Alan Shearer	260	441	1992-2006
2 Wayne Rooney	208	491	2002-18
3 Andrew Cole	187	414	1993-2008
4 Sergio Aguero	184	275	2011-21
5 Frank Lampard	177	609	1996-2015
6 Thierry Henry	175	258	1999-2012
7 Harry Kane	166	245	2012-present
8 Robbie Fowler	163	379	1993-2008
9 Jermain Defoe	162	496	2001-18
10 Michael Owen	150	326	1997-2013

ALAN SHEARER

The iconic No.9 was the first player to score 200 Premier League goals – and he's the only player to score 100 goals for two separate clubs (Newcastle and Blackburn). Big Al also scored the most Prem penalties (56) and the most goals from inside the penalty box – 227!

HARRY KANE

The England striker holds the record for the most Prem goals scored in a calendar year – he bagged 39 for Tottenham in 2017. Also, no-one has a better strike rate than Kane, who averages a goal every 1.47 games!

SERGIO AGUERO

The Man. City legend holds the record for the most Premier League goals by a foreign player and he also holds the record for most Prem hat-tricks with 12 – one more than Alan Shearer!

GOAL KINGS

YOUNGEST PLAYERS TO REACH 100 GOALS

PLAYER	AGE WHEN SCORED 100TH GOAL
1 Michael Owen	23 years, 133 days
2 Robbie Fowler	23 years, 282 days
3 Wayne Rooney	24 years, 99 days
4 Harry Kane	24 years, 191 days
5 Romelu Lukaku	24 years, 322 days

YOUNGEST GOAL SCORER
JAMES VAUGHAN
16 years, 270 days
Everton v Crystal
Palace, 2005

MICHAEL OWEN
Owen exploded onto the scene as a 17-year-old wonderkid for Liverpool in 1997 and it took him just 185 games to hit 100 Prem goals for the Reds. After one season playing for Real Madrid in 2004-05 he returned to England, appearing for Newcastle, Man. United and Stoke!

OLDEST GOAL SCORER
TEDDY SHERINGHAM
40 years, 268 days
West Ham v
Portsmouth, 2006

PREMIER LEAGUE

MOST GOALS IN A SEASON

34

ANDREW COLE
Newcastle
1993-94
(42 matches)

ALAN SHEARER
Blackburn
1994-95
(42 matches)

32

MOHAMED SALAH
Liverpool
2017-18
(38 matches)

DID YOU KNOW? At the end of the 1994–95 season, the league was reduced from 22 teams to 20, resulting in four fewer matches for each club!

MOST GOALS IN A SINGLE MATCH

5

ANDREW COLE
Man. United v Ipswich, 1994-95
ALAN SHEARER
Newcastle v Sheffield
Wednesday, 1999-2000
JERMAIN DEFOE
Tottenham v Wigan, 2009-10
DIMITAR BERBATOV
Man. United v Blackburn, 2010-11
SERGIO AGUERO
Man. City v Newcastle, 2015-16

MOST CONSECUTIVE MATCHES SCORED IN

11

JAMIE VARDY
Leicester, 2015-16

GOAL KINGS

MOST FREE-KICKS SCORED

1 David Beckham	18
2= Gianfranco Zola	12
2= Thierry Henry	12
4= Laurent Robert	11
4= Cristiano Ronaldo	11
4= Sebastian Larsson	11

MOST CLUBS SCORED FOR

7 CRAIG BELLAMY
Coventry, Newcastle, Blackburn, Liverpool, West Ham, Man. City & Cardiff, 2000-14

MOST GOALS FROM OUTSIDE THE BOX

41

FRANK LAMPARD Frank is also the Premier League's top-scoring midfielder!

FASTEST GOAL

SHANE LONG 7.69 seconds
Watford v Southampton, 24 April 2019

MOST HEADED GOALS

53 PETER CROUCH
Aston Villa, Southampton, Liverpool, Portsmouth, Tottenham & Stoke 2001-18

FASTEST HAT-TRICK

SADIO MANE
2 minutes, 56 seconds
Southampton
v Aston Villa,
16 May 2015

PREMIER LEAGUE

PREMIER LEAGUE KEEPERS

MOST CLEAN SHEETS

PLAYER	CLEAN SHEETS	YEARS
1 Petr Cech	202	2004-19
2 David James	169	1992-2010
3 Mark Schwarzer	151	1996-2015
4 David Seaman	141	1992-2004
5 Nigel Martyn	137	1992-2006

MOST CLEAN SHEETS IN A ROW

14

EDWIN VAN DER SAR
Man. United, 2008-09

MOST PENALTIES SAVED

13

DAVID JAMES
Liverpool, Man. City & Portsmouth 1992-2010

MOST PLAYER OF THE YEAR AWARDS

2

THIERRY HENRY
Arsenal, 2003-04 & 2005-06

CRISTIANO RONALDO
Man. United, 2006-07 & 2007-08

NEMANJA VIDIC
Man. United, 2008-09 & 2010-11

RECORD BREAKERS

OLDEST PLAYER

JOHN BURRIDGE
43 years, 162 days
Man. City v QPR, 1994-95

YOUNGEST PLAYER

HARVEY ELLIOTT
16 years, 30 days
Wolves v **Fulham**, 2018-19

MOST RED CARDS

8

DUNCAN FERGUSON
Everton &
Newcastle,
1994-2006

RICHARD DUNNE
Everton, Man. City, Aston
Villa & QPR, 1996-2015

PATRICK VIEIRA
Arsenal & Man. City,
1996-2011

HIGHEST-SCORING MATCH

PORTSMOUTH **7-4** READING
Fratton Park, 2007-08

HIGHEST ATTENDANCE

83,222
TOTTENHAM V ARSENAL
Wembley Stadium, 2017-18

HIGHEST SEASON AVERAGE ATTENDANCE

75,821
Man. United, Old Trafford
2006-07

LOWEST ATTENDANCE

3,039
Wimbledon v Everton
Selhurst Park, 1992-93

BIGGEST WIN

9-0

MAN. UNITED 9-0 IPSWICH
Old Trafford, 1994-95

SOUTHAMPTON 0-9 LEICESTER
St Mary's Stadium, 2019-20

MAN. UNITED 9-0 SOUTHAMPTON
Old Trafford, 2020-21

 ENGLAND

The Premier League may have launched in 1992, but there has been league football in England for more than 130 years. Let's take a look at some of the records set and smashed in that time!

ALL TIME LIST OF TITLE WINNERS

CLUB	TITLE WINS	LEAGUE TITLES
1 Man. United	20	1907-08, 1910-11, 1951-52, 1955-56, 1956-57, 1964-65, 1966-67, 1992-93, 1993-94, 1995-96, 1996-97, 1998-99, 1999-2000, 2000-01, 2002-03, 2006-07, 2007-08, 2008-09, 2010-11, 2012-13
2 Liverpool	19	1900-01, 1905-06, 1921-22, 1922-23, 1946-47, 1963-64, 1965-66, 1972-73, 1975-76, 1976-77, 1978-79, 1979-80, 1981-82, 1982-83, 1983-84, 1985-86, 1987-88, 1989-90, 2019-20
3 Arsenal	13	1930-31, 1932-33, 1933-34, 1934-35, 1937-38, 1947-48, 1952-53, 1970-71, 1988-89, 1990-91, 1997-98, 2001-02, 2003-04
4 Everton	9	1890-91, 1914-15, 1927-28, 1931-32, 1938-39, 1962-63, 1969-70, 1984-85, 1986-87
5= Aston Villa	7	1893-94, 1895-96, 1896-97, 1898-99, 1899-1900, 1909-10, 1980-81
5= Man. City	7	1936-37, 1967-68, 2011-12, 2013-14, 2017-18, 2018-19, 2020-21
7= Sunderland	6	1891-92, 1892-93, 1894-95, 1901-02, 1912-13, 1935-36
7= Chelsea	6	1954-55, 2004-05, 2005-06, 2009-10, 2014-15, 2016-17
9= Newcastle	4	1904-05, 1906-07, 1908-09, 1926-27
9= Sheffield Wednesday	4	1902-03, 1903-04, 1928-29, 1929-30

Super Reds Liverpool won the title TEN times in 14 years between 1976 and 1990!

MOST GOALS IN ENGLISH FOOTBALL

434

ARTHUR ROWLEY West Brom, Fulham, Leicester & Shrewsbury, 1946-65

MOST SEASONS IN ENGLISH TOP-FLIGHT

118

EVERTON

BIGGEST LEAGUE WIN

13-0

Stockport 13-0 Halifax
Third Division North, 1933-34

Newcastle 13-0 Newport
Second Division, 1946-47

MOST GOALS IN A GAME

17

Tranmere 13-4 Oldham
Third Division North, 1935-36

MOST LEAGUE GOALS IN A SEASON

60

DIXIE DEAN Everton, 1927-28

MOST GOALS IN A GAME

10

JOE PAYNE
Luton 12-0 Bristol Rovers, 1935-36

MOST LEAGUE APPEARANCES

1,005

PETER SHILTON
Leicester, Stoke, Nottingham Forest,
Southampton, Derby, Plymouth,
Wimbledon, Bolton, Coventry, West
Ham, Leyton Orient, 1966-97

ENGLAND

THE FOOTBALL PYRAMID

1 — **PREMIER LEAGUE** 20 clubs

2 — **EFL CHAMPIONSHIP** 24 clubs

3 — **EFL LEAGUE ONE** 24 clubs

4 — **EFL LEAGUE TWO** 24 clubs

5 — **NATIONAL LEAGUE** 22 clubs

6 — National League North 22 clubs / National League South 22 clubs

7 — Northern League Premier Division 22 clubs / Southern League South Division 22 clubs / Southern League Central Division 22 clubs / Isthmian League Premier Division 22 clubs

Below level 7 are more than 100 regional leagues that make up the rest of the pyramid.

The English league system, or the football pyramid, is a series of leagues connected by promotion and relegation from one to the other.

■ There are more than 140 individual leagues, containing more than 480 divisions, and more than 40,000 clubs in England. As well as all the English clubs, there are five teams from Wales, one from Guernsey, one from Jersey and one from the Isle Of Man.

THE CHAMPIONSHIP

Number of clubs 24 **Promotion to** Premier League **Relegation to** League One **2020-21 champions** Norwich **2020-21 top scorer** Ivan Toney, Brentford, 31 goals

BIGGEST STADIUMS

1 Riverside, Middlesbrough **34,742**

2 Pride Park, Derby **33,597**

3 Cardiff City Stadium, Cardiff **33,316**

MOST SUCCESSFUL CLUB

BLACKBURN
3 league titles
6 FA Cup wins

LEAGUE ONE

Number of clubs 24 **Promotion to** The Championship **Relegation to** League Two **2020-21 champions** Hull **2020-21 top scorer** Jonson Clarke-Harris, Peterborough, 31 goals

Biggest stadiums

1 Stadium of Light, Sunderland **49,000**

2 Hillsborough, Sheffield Wednesday **39,732**

3 Stadium MK, MK Dons **30,500**

Most successful club
Sunderland 6 league titles, 2 FA Cup wins

LEAGUE TWO

Number of clubs 24 **Promotion to** League One **Relegation to** National League **2020-21 champions** Cheltenham **2020-21 top scorer** Paul Mullin, Cambridge, 32 goals

Biggest stadiums

1 Valley Parade, Bradford, **25,136**

2 Vale Park, Port Vale **19,052**

3 Brunton Park, Carlisle **18,202**

Most successful club
Bradford 1 FA Cup win

THE FA CUP

The Football Association Challenge Cup, to give it its full name, is an annual knockout competition in English football. It was first played during the 1871-72 season, making it the oldest national football competition in the world!

FACT FILE

Organising body The Football Association
Founded 1871, 150 years ago
Region England & Wales
Competing clubs 736 (2020–21)

WHO ARE THE MOST SUCCESSFUL CLUBS IN FA CUP HISTORY?

CLUB	WINS	RUNNERS-UP	TOTAL FINALS
1 Arsenal	14	7	21
2 Man. United	12	8	20
3= Chelsea	8	7	15
3= Tottenham	8	1	9
5= Liverpool	7	7	14
5= Aston Villa	7	4	11
7= Newcastle	6	7	13
7= Man. City	6	5	11
7= Blackburn	6	2	8
10 Everton	5	8	13

BIGGEST WIN IN AN FA CUP FINAL

Bury **6–0** Derby (1903)
Man. City **6–0** Watford (2019)

MOST FA CUP WINS BY A PLAYER

7

ASHLEY COLE

The ledge England left-back won it with Arsenal in 2002, 2003 and 2005, before moving to Chelsea and winning it in 2007, 2009, 2010 and 2012!

MOST FINALS SCORED IN

4

DIDIER DROGBA

Drogba, another Chelsea hero, netted in four FA Cup finals – 2007, 2009, 2010 and 2012 – helping himself to four FA Cup winner's medals in the process!

BIGGEST WIN IN FA CUP HISTORY

Preston **26–0** Hyde (first round, 1887)

Emirates FA CUP

The official attendance was 126,047, but many people believe the 1923 final crowd was closer to 300,000!

THE BIGGEST CROWD FOR A FA CUP FINAL

126,047

Bolton 2-0 West Ham, Wembley, 1923

FIVE BIG CUP FACTS

■ Forty-four different clubs have won the FA Cup since it began 150 years ago
■ Cardiff are the only non-English club to have won the competition
■ West Ham were the first club from outside the top division to win it when they beat Arsenal 1-0 in the 1980 final

■ In 2013, Wigan became the first club to win the FA Cup and be relegated from the top-flight in the same season – they're still the only club to do that
■ Brendan Rodgers became the first British manager to lift the cup for 13 years when Leicester won it in 2020-21

SCOTLAND

1985
The last time a club other than Celtic or Rangers were Scottish champions was 36 years ago, when Aberdeen lifted the trophy!

11-0
The biggest win in the Scottish top flight came in 1895 when Celtic put 11 past Dundee!

118,567
The highest attendance was, unsurprisingly, for an Old Firm game at Ibrox between Rangers and Celtic way back in 1939!

410
Ex-Celtic striker Jimmy McGrory scored a record 410 top-flight goals between 1922 and 1937 – he once scored eight goals in a game!

SCOTTISH SUPERCLUBS

RANGERS

Founded 1872 (149 years ago) **Stadium** Ibrox Stadium **Capacity** 50,817
Manager Steven Gerrard **Star player** Connor Goldson **Club icons**
Ally McCoist, John Greig, Jim Baxter, Davie Cooper, Brian Laudrup

CELTIC

Founded 1887 (133 years ago) **Stadium** Celtic Park **Capacity** 60,411
Star player Odsonne Eduoard **Club icons** Kenny Dalglish,
Henrik Larsson, Jimmy Johnstone, Billy McNeill, Paul McStay

Manager role vacant at the time of going to press

SPAIN

THE COUNTRY

Population 47 million
Area 505,990 km² **Currency** Euro
Capital Madrid (3.3 million)
Other major cities Barcelona, Valencia, Seville

LA LIGA

Full name Campeonato Nacional De Liga De Primera Division
Founded 1929 (92 years ago)
Number of clubs 20 **Domestic cups** Copa Del Rey, Supercopa De Espana
Website laliga.es

BIGGEST STADIUMS

1	2	3
Nou Camp	**Santiago Bernabeu**	**Wanda Metropolitano**
Barcelona 99,354	Real Madrid 81,044	A. Madrid 68,456

BEST PLAYER OF ALL TIME

LIONEL MESSI, Barcelona, 2004-present

MOST LEAGUE TITLES

1 Real Madrid	34
2 Barcelona	26
3 Atletico Madrid	11
4 Athletic Bilbao	8
5 Valencia	6

MOST LA LIGA GOALS

1. LIONEL MESSI
Barcelona 2004-present, **475 goals**

2 CRISTIANO RONALDO
Real Madrid 2009-18, **311 goals**

3 TELMO ZARRA
Athletic Bilbao 1940-55, **251 goals**

MOST LA LIGA APPEARANCES

1 ANDONI ZUBIZARRETA Athletic Bilbao, Barcelona, Valencia, 1981-98, **622 games**

2 JOAQUIN Real Betis, Valencia, Malaga 2001-present, **578 games**

3 RAUL Real Madrid, 1994-2010, **550 games**

MOST EXPENSIVE SIGNING

£144m

PHILIPPE COUTINHO
Liverpool to Barca, 2018

LaLiga

REAL MADRID

Founded 1902 (119 years ago) **Stadium** Santiago Bernabeu **Capacity** 81,044
Head coach Carlo Ancelotti **Star player** Sergio Ramos **Club icons** Raul,
Alfredo Di Stefano, Cristiano Ronaldo, Iker Casillas, Ferenc Puskas

BARCELONA

Founded 1899 (121 years ago) **Stadium** Nou Camp **Capacity** 99,354 **Head coach**
Ronald Koeman **Star player** Lionel Messi **Club icons** Johan Cruyff, Xavi, Andres Iniesta,
Ronaldinho, Ladislao Kubala

ITALY

THE COUNTRY
Population 60 million
Area 301,340 km²
Currency Euro
Capital Rome (2.9 million)
Other major cities Milan, Naples, Turin

SERIE A
Full name Serie A
Founded 1898 (122 years ago)
Number of clubs 20
Domestic cups Coppa Italia, Supercoppa Italiana
Website legaseriea.it

BIGGEST STADIUMS
1 San Siro
AC Milan & Inter Milan, 75,923

2 Stadio Olimpico
Roma & Lazio, 70,634

3 Stadio San Paolo
Napoli, 54,726

BEST PLAYER OF ALL TIME
DIEGO MARADONA Napoli, 1984-1991

MOST LEAGUE TITLES
1 Juventus	36
2 Inter Milan	19
3 AC Milan	18
4 Genoa	9
5 Torino, Bologna & Pro Vercelli	7

MOST SERIE A GOALS

1 SILVIO PIOLA Pro Vercelli, Lazio, Juventus & Novara, 1929-54 **274 goals**

2 FRANCESCO TOTTI Roma, 1992-2017 **250 goals**

3 GUNNAR NORDAHL AC Milan & Roma, 1949-58 **225 goals**

MOST EXPENSIVE SIGNING

£99m
CRISTIANO RONALDO Real Madrid to Juventus, 2018

SERIE A
TIM

MOST SERIE A APPEARANCES

1 GIANLUIGI BUFFON
Parma, Juventus
1995-present, **656 games**

2 PAOLO MALDINI
AC Milan, 1984-2009,
647 games

3 FRANCESCO TOTTI
Roma, 1992-2017,
619 games

SERIE A SUPERCLUB

JUVENTUS

Founded 1897 (123 years ago) **Stadium** Juventus Stadium **Capacity** 41,507 **Head coach** Massimiliano Allegri **Star player** Cristiano Ronaldo **Club icons** Alessandro Del Piero, Roberto Baggio, Zinedine Zidane, Michel Platini, John Charles

GERMANY

THE COUNTRY

Population 83 million
Area 357,022 km² **Currency** Euro
Capital Berlin (3.8 million)
Other major cities Munich,
Hamburg, Cologne

BUNDESLIGA

Full name 1. Bundesliga
Founded 1963 (57 years ago)
Number of clubs 18
Domestic cups DFB-Pokal,
DFL-Supercup
Website Bundesliga.com

BIGGEST STADIUM

Westfalenstadion
Borussia Dortmund, 81,365

BEST PLAYER OF ALL TIME

FRANZ BECKENBAUER
Bayern Munich & Hamburg, 1964-82

MOST LEAGUE TITLES

1 Bayern Munich		30
2 Borussia Dortmund		5
3 B. Monchengladbach		5
4 Werder Bremen		4
5 Hamburg & Stuttgart		3

BUNDESLIGA SUPERCLUB

BAYERN MUNICH Founded 1900
(121 years ago) **Stadium** Allianz Arena
Capacity 75,000 **Head coach** Julian
Nagelsmann **Star player** Robert
Lewandowski **Club icons** Franz
Beckenbauer, Gerd Muller, Karl-Heinz
Rummenigge, Lothar Matthaus,
Philipp Lahm

MOST BUNDESLIGA GOALS

365

Gerd Muller
Bayern Munich,
1965-79

MOST BUNDESLIGA APPEARANCES

Karl-Heinz Korbel
Eintracht Frankfurt, 1972-91 **602 games**

FRANCE

THE COUNTRY

Population 67 million
Area 640,679 km² **Currency** Euro
Capital Paris (2.2 million)
Other major cities Marseille,
Lyon, Toulouse

LIGUE 1

Full name Ligue 1
Founded 1930 (90 years ago)
Number of clubs 20
Domestic cups Coupe de France,
Trophee des Champions
Website ligue1.com

BIGGEST STADIUM

Stade Velodrome
Marseille, 67,394

BEST PLAYER OF ALL TIME

MICHEL PLATINI
Nancy & Saint-Etienne, 1972-82

MOST LEAGUE TITLES

1 Saint-Etienne	10
2= Marseille	9
2= PSG	9
4= Monaco	8
4= Nantes	8

LIGUE 1 SUPERCLUB

PSG Founded 1970 (50 years ago)
Stadium Parc des Princes **Capacity**
47,929 **Head coach** Mauricio Pochettino
Star player Kylian Mbappe **Club icons**
Safet Susic, Edinson Cavani, Zlatan
Ibrahimovic, Ronaldinho, Rai

MOST LIGUE 1 GOALS

299

Delio Onnis
Monaco, Reims,
Tours & Toulon,
1972-86

MOST LIGUE 1 APPEARANCES

Mickael Landreau, Nantes, PSG, Lille
& Bastia, 1997-2014 **618 games**

PORTUGAL

LIGA NOS

THE COUNTRY

Population 10.3m **Area** 92,226 km²
Currency Euro **Capital** Lisbon (2.6m)
Major cities Porto, Braga, Coimbra

PORTUGUESE PRIMEIRA LIGA

Founded 1934 **Number of clubs** 18
Domestic cups Taca De Portugal,
Supertaca
Website ligaportugal.pt

BIGGEST STADIUM

Estadio Da Luz Benfica, 64,642

MOST LEAGUE TITLES

1 Benfica		37
2 Porto		29
3 Sporting Lisbon		19
4= Belenenses		1
4= Boavista		1

BEST PLAYER OF ALL TIME

EUSEBIO
Benfica &
Beira-Mar,
1960-77

HOLLAND

eredivisie

THE COUNTRY

Population 17.5m **Area** 41,865 km²
Currency Euro **Capital** Amsterdam (872k)
Major cities Rotterdam, The Hague,
Utrecht

EREDIVISIE

Founded 1956 **Number of clubs** 18
Domestic cups KNVB Cup, Johan Cruyff
Shield **Website** eredivisie.nl

BIGGEST STADIUM

Johan Cruyff Arena Ajax Amsterdam, 55,000

MOST LEAGUE TITLES

1 Ajax		35
2 PSV		24
3 Feyenoord		15
4 Den Haag		10
5 Sparta Rotterdam		6

BEST PLAYER OF ALL TIME

**JOHAN
CRUYFF**
Ajax &
Feyenoord,
1964-84

ARGENTINA

THE COUNTRY

Population 45m **Area** 2,780,400 km²
Currency Peso **Capital** Buenos Aires
(15.5m) **Major cities** Cordoba, Rosario,
Mendoza

ARGENTINE PRIMERA DIVISION

Founded 1891 **Number of clubs** 24
Domestic cups Copa Argentina, Supercopa
Argentina **Website** ligaprofesional.org.ar

BIGGEST STADIUM

El Monumental River Plate, 70,074

MOST LEAGUE TITLES

1 River Plate		36
2 Boca Juniors		34
3 Racing Club		18
4 Independiente		16
5 San Lorenzo		15

BEST PLAYER OF ALL TIME

DIEGO MARADONA
Argentinos Juniors, Boca Juniors & Newell's Old Boys, 1976-97

BRAZIL

THE COUNTRY

Population 210m **Area** 8,515,767 km²
Currency Real **Capital** Brasilia (3m)
Major cities Rio De Janeiro, Sao Paulo,
Salvador

CAMPEONATO BRASILEIRO SERIE A

Founded 1959 **Number of clubs** 20
Domestic cups Copa Do Brasil, Supercopa
Do Brasil **Website** brasileirao.cbf.com.br

BIGGEST STADIUM

Maracana Stadium Flamengo
& Fluminense, 78,838

MOST LEAGUE TITLES

1 Palmeiras		10
2 Santos		8
3= Corinthians		7
3= Flamengo		7
5 Sao Paulo		6

BEST PLAYER OF ALL TIME

PELE
Santos
1956-74

THE TOP CLUBS FROM

EUROPE		
COUNTRY	**LEAGUE NAME**	**MOST SUCCESSFUL CLUB**
Austria	Austrian Football Bundesliga	Rapid Vienna **32 titles**
Azerbaijan	Azerbaijan Premier League	Neftchi Baku **9 titles**
Belarus	Belarusian Premier League	BATE Borisov **15 titles**
Belgium	Belgian First Division A	Anderlecht **34 titles**
Bulgaria	Bulgarian First League	CSKA Sofia **31 titles**
Croatia	Croatian First Football League	Dinamo Zagreb **31 titles***
Cyprus	Cypriot First Division	APOEL **28 titles**
Czech Republic	Czech First League	Sparta Prague **36 titles***
Denmark	Danish Superliga	Copenhagen **13 titles**
Greece	Super League Greece	Olympiakos **46 titles**
Israel	Israeli Premier League	Maccabi Tel Aviv **23 titles**
Kazakhstan	Kazakh Premier League	Astana **6 titles**
Northern Ireland	NIFL Premiership	Linfield **55 titles**
Norway	Eliteserien	Rosenborg **26 titles**
Poland	Ekstraklasa	Legia Warsaw **15 titles**
Rep. Of Ireland	League Of Ireland Premier Division	Shamrock Rovers **18 titles**
Romania	Liga 1	FCSB **26 titles**
Russia	Russian Premier League	Spartak Moscow **22 titles***
Serbia	Serbian SuperLiga	Red Star Belgrade **32 titles***
Slovakia	Slovak Super Liga	Slovan Bratislava **23 titles***
Sweden	Allsvenskan	Malmo **24 titles**
Switzerland	Swiss Super League	Grasshoppers **27 titles**
Turkey	Super Lig	Galatasaray **22 titles**
Ukraine	Ukrainian Premier League	Dynamo Kiev **29 titles***
Wales	Cymru Premier	The New Saints **13 titles**

*Includes title wins in former states

AROUND THE WORLD

NORTH & CENTRAL AMERICA		
COUNTRY	**LEAGUE NAME**	**MOST SUCCESSFUL CLUB**
Mexico	Mexico Liga MX	America **13 titles**
USA	MLS	LA Galaxy **5 titles**

SOUTH AMERICA		
COUNTRY	**LEAGUE NAME**	**MOST SUCCESSFUL CLUB**
Chile	**Chilean Primera Division**	**Colo-Colo 32 titles**
Colombia	Categoria Primera A	Atletico Nacional **16 titles**
Ecuador	**Ecuadorian Serie A**	**Barcelona SC 16 titles**
Peru	Peruvian Primera Division	Universitario **26 titles**
Uruguay	**Uruguayan Primera Division**	**Penarol 50 titles**

ASIA		
COUNTRY	**LEAGUE NAME**	**MOST SUCCESSFUL CLUB**
Australia	**A-League**	**Sydney FC 5 titles**
China	Chinese Super League	Guangzhou **8 titles** Dalian Shide **8 titles**
India	**Indian Super League / I-League**	**Mohan Bagan 5 titles Dempo 5 titles**
Japan	J1 League	Kashima Antlers **8 titles**
South Korea	**K League 1**	**Jeonbuk HM 8 titles**

AFRICA		
COUNTRY	**LEAGUE NAME**	**MOST SUCCESSFUL CLUB**
Algeria	Ligue 1	JS Kabylie **14 titles**
DR Congo	Linafoot	TP Mazembe **17 titles**
Egypt	**Egyptian Premier League**	**Al Ahly 42 titles**
Morocco	Botola Pro	Wydad Casablanca **20 titles**
South Africa	**South African Premier Division**	**Mamelodi Sundowns 13 titles**
Tunisia	Ligue 1	Esperance De Tunis **31 titles**

THE CHAMPIONS

The UEFA Champions League is, quite simply, the most prestigious club competition in the world, featuring the biggest teams and the best players.

It began life back in 1955-56 as the European Cup, which was a straight knockout competition for the champions of Europe's leagues. But in 1992, it was rebranded and took on its current name.

Now, title winners from across Europe are joined by a number of runners-up from the stronger leagues. These 32 teams compete in an initial group stage before qualifying for the knockout phase, which ultimately ends with a nail-biting, drama-filled final.

Spanish clubs have been the most successful (18 wins), followed by English (14 wins) and then Italian (12 wins) – although England has spread its victories between the most teams, with five different clubs claiming the title.

LEAGUE

Real Madrid won the first FIVE European Cup finals, from 1955-56 to 1959-60. Here they are in 1956, before beating French club Reims 4-3 to claim their first trophy!

Marseille celebrate becoming the very first winners of the renamed Champions League in 1993 after beating AC Milan 1-0!

The most dramatic UCL final saw Man. United score two injury-time goals to beat Bayern Munich 2-1 in 1999!

CHAMPIONS LEAGUE

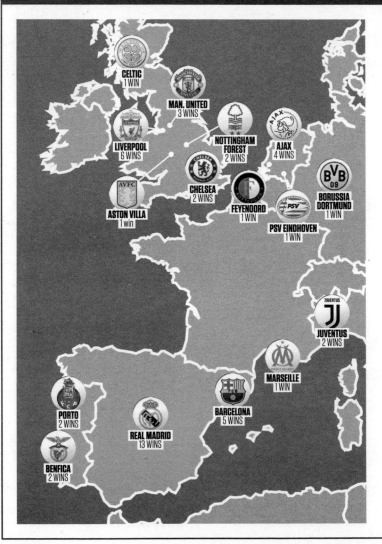

CELTIC
1 WIN

MAN. UNITED
3 WINS

LIVERPOOL
6 WINS

NOTTINGHAM
FOREST
2 WINS

AJAX
4 WINS

CHELSEA
2 WINS

FEYENOORD
1 WIN

BORUSSIA
DORTMUND
1 WIN

ASTON VILLA
1 win

PSV EINDHOVEN
1 WIN

JUVENTUS
2 WINS

MARSEILLE
1 WIN

PORTO
2 WINS

BARCELONA
5 WINS

REAL MADRID
13 WINS

BENFICA
2 WINS

WINNERS

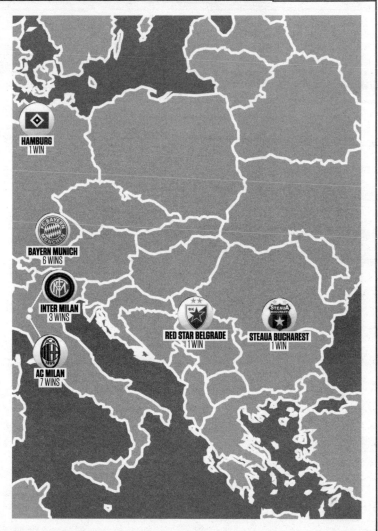

HAMBURG
1 WIN

BAYERN MUNICH
6 WINS

INTER MILAN
3 WINS

AC MILAN
7 WINS

RED STAR BELGRADE
1 WIN

STEAUA BUCHAREST
1 WIN

CHAMPIONS OF

CLUB	COUNTRY	WINS	YEARS
Real Madrid	**Spain**	**13**	**1956, 1957, 1958, 1959, 1960, 1966, 1998, 2000, 2002, 2014, 2016, 2017, 2018**
AC Milan	Italy	7	1963, 1969, 1989, 1990, 1994, 2003, 2007
Bayern Munich	**Germany**	**6**	**1974, 1975, 1976, 2001, 2013, 2020**
Liverpool	England	6	1977, 1978, 1981, 1984, 2005, 2019
Barcelona	**Spain**	**5**	**1992, 2006, 2009, 2011, 2015**
Ajax	Holland	4	1971, 1972, 1973, 1995
Man. United	**England**	**3**	**1968, 1999, 2008**
Inter Milan	Italy	3	1964, 1965, 2010
Juventus	**Italy**	**2**	**1985, 1996**
Benfica	Portugal	2	1961, 1962
Nottingham Forest	**England**	**2**	**1979, 1980**
Porto	Portugal	2	1987, 2004
Chelsea	**England**	**2**	**2012 , 2021**
Celtic	Scotland	1	1967
Hamburg	**Germany**	**1**	**1983**
Steaua Bucharest	Romania	1	1986
Marseille	**France**	**1**	**1993**
Borussia Dortmund	Germany	1	1997
Feyenoord	**Holland**	**1**	**1970**
Aston Villa	England	1	1982
PSV	**Holland**	**1**	**1988**
Red Star Belgrade	Serbia	1	1991

EUROPE

Real Madrid are the only club in the Champions League era to successfully defend their title – in fact, their win in 2018 was their third in a row!

Liverpool's six wins make them the most successful British club in the competition's history!

Legendary manager Brian Clough and his assistant Peter Taylor led Nottingham Forest to shock European glory in 1979 and 1980!

UCL FINALS AND

Since the European Cup became the Champions League way back in 1992, there have been 29 epic finals full of drama, excitement and momentous moments. Here's what happened in EVERY ONE of those finals!

1992-93

MARSEILLE 1–0 AC MILAN

Boli 43

VENUE Olympiastadion, Munich, Germany ATTENDANCE 64,400

1993-94

AC MILAN 4–0 BARCELONA

Massaro 22, 45,
Savicevic 47, Desailly 58

VENUE Olympic Stadium, Athens, Greece ATTENDANCE 70,000

1994-95

AJAX 1–0 AC MILAN

Kluivert 85

VENUE Ernst-Happel-Stadion, Vienna, Austria ATTENDANCE 49,730

1995-96

JUVENTUS 1–1 (AET) AJAX

Ravanelli 13   **JUVENTUS WON 4-2 ON PENALTIES**   Litmanen 41

VENUE Stadio Olimpico, Rome, Italy ATTENDANCE 70,000

1996-97

B. DORTMUND 3–1 JUVENTUS

Riedle 29, 34,
Ricken 71   Del Piero 65

VENUE Olympiastadion, Munich, Germany ATTENDANCE 59,000

1997-98

REAL MADRID 1–0 JUVENTUS

Mijatovic 66

VENUE Amsterdam Arena, Amsterdam, Holland ATTENDANCE 48,500

1998-99

MAN. UNITED 2–1 BAYERN MUNICH

Sheringham 90,
Solskjaer 90   Basler 6

VENUE Nou Camp, Barcelona, Spain ATTENDANCE 90,245

WINNERS

1999-2000

REAL MADRID **3–0** VALENCIA

Morientes 39,
McManaman 67, Raul 75

VENUE Stade De France, Saint-Denis, France **ATTENDANCE** 80,000

2000-01

BAYERN MUNICH **1–1** (AET) VALENCIA

Effenberg 50 (pen)   **BAYERN WON 5-4 ON PENALTIES**   Mendieta 3 (pen)

VENUE San Siro, Milan, Italy **ATTENDANCE** 79,000

2001-02

REAL MADRID **2–1** BAYER LEVERKUSEN

Raul 8,
Zidane 45   Lucio 13

VENUE Hampden Park, Glasgow, Scotland **ATTENDANCE** 50,499

2002-03

AC MILAN **0–0** (AET) JUVENTUS

AC MILAN WON 3-2 ON PENALTIES

VENUE Old Trafford, Manchester, England **ATTENDANCE** 62,315

2003-04

PORTO **3–0** MONACO

Carlos Alberto 39,
Deco 71, Alenichev 75

VENUE Arena AufSchalke, Gelsenkirchen, Germany **ATTENDANCE** 53,053

2005-06

BARCELONA **2–1** ARSENAL

Eto'o 76,
Belletti 80   Campbell 37

VENUE Stade De France, Saint-Denis, France **ATTENDANCE** 79,610

2004-05

LIVERPOOL **3–3** (AET) AC MILAN

Gerrard 54, Smicer
56, Alonso 60   **LIVERPOOL WON 3-2 ON PENALTIES**   Maldini 1, Crespo 39, 44

VENUE Ataturk Olympic Stadium, Istanbul, Turkey **ATTENDANCE** 69,000

UCL FINALS AND

2006-07

AC MILAN 2–1 LIVERPOOL

Inzaghi 45, 82   Kuyt 89

VENUE Olympic Stadium, Athens, Greece **ATTENDANCE** 63,000

2007-08

MAN. UNITED 1–1 (AET) CHELSEA

Ronaldo 26   **MAN. UNITED WON 6–5 ON PENALTIES**   Lampard 45

VENUE Luzhniki Stadium, Moscow, Russia **ATTENDANCE** 67,310

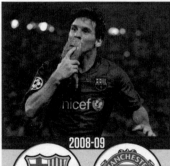

2009-10

INTER MILAN 2–0 BAYERN MUNICH

Milito 35, 70

VENUE Santiago Bernabeu, Madrid, Spain **ATTENDANCE** 73,490

2008-09

BARCELONA 2–0 MAN. UNITED

Eto'o 10,
Messi 70

VENUE Stadio Olimpico, Rome, Italy **ATTENDANCE** 62,467

2010-11

BARCELONA 3–1 MAN. UNITED

Pedro 27,   Rooney 34
Messi 54, Villa 69

VENUE Wembley Stadium, London, England **ATTENDANCE** 87,695

2011-12

CHELSEA 1–1 (AET) BAYERN MUNICH

Drogba 88   **CHELSEA WON 4–3 ON PENALTIES**   Muller 83

VENUE Allianz Arena, Munich, Germany **ATTENDANCE** 62,500

2012-13

BAYERN MUNICH 2–1 B. DORTMUND

Mandzukic 60,   Gundogan 68 (pen)
Robben 89

VENUE Wembley Stadium, London, England **ATTENDANCE** 86,298

WINNERS

2013-14

REAL MADRID **4–1** (AET) ATLETICO MADRID

Ramos 90, Bale 110,   Godin 36
Marcelo 118, Ronaldo 120 (pen)

VENUE Estadio Da Luz, Lisbon, Portugal **ATTENDANCE** 60,976

2014-15

BARCELONA **3–1** JUVENTUS

Rakitic 4, Suarez 68,   Morata 55
Neymar 90

VENUE Olympiastadion, Berlin, Germany **ATTENDANCE** 70,442

2015-16

REAL MADRID **1–1** (AET) ATLETICO MADRID

Ramos 15   **REAL MADRID WON**   Carrasco 79
            5-3 ON PENALTIES

VENUE San Siro, Milan, Italy **ATTENDANCE** 71,942

2016-17

REAL MADRID **4–1** JUVENTUS

Ronaldo 20, 64,   Mandzukic 27
Casemiro 61, Asensio 90

VENUE Millennium Stadium, Cardiff, Wales **ATTENDANCE** 65,842

2017-18

REAL MADRID **3–1** LIVERPOOL

Benzema 51,   Mane 55
Bale 63, 83

VENUE NSC Olimpiyskiy Stadium, Kiev, Ukraine **ATTENDANCE** 61,561

2018-19

LIVERPOOL **2–0** TOTTENHAM

Salah 2 (pen),
Origi 87

VENUE Metropolitano Stadium, Madrid, Spain **ATTENDANCE** 63,272

2019-20

BAYERN MUNICH **1–0** PSG

Coman 59

VENUE Estadio Da Luz, Lisbon, Portugal **ATTENDANCE** No fans present

2020-21

CHELSEA **1-0** MAN. CITY

Havertz 42

VENUE Estadio Do Dragao, Porto, Portugal **ATTENDANCE** 14,110

TOP 20 CHAMPIONS LEAGUE & EUROPEAN CUP GOAL SCORERS OF ALL TIME

PLAYER	GOALS	GAMES	YEARS	CLUB(S)
1 Cristiano Ronaldo	134	176	2003-present	Man. United, Real Madrid, Juventus
2 Lionel Messi	120	149	2005-present	Barcelona
3 Robert Lewandowski	73	96	2011-present	B. Dortmund, Bayern Munich
4= Karim Benzema	71	130	2006-present	Lyon, Real Madrid
4= Raul	71	142	1995-2011	Real Madrid, Schalke
6 Ruud van Nistelrooy	56	73	1998-2009	PSV, Man. United, Real Madrid
7 Thierry Henry	50	112	1997-2012	Monaco, Arsenal, Barcelona
8 Alfredo Di Stefano	49	58	1955-64	Real Madrid
9= Andriy Shevchenko	48	100	1994-2012	Dynamo Kiev, AC Milan, Chelsea
9= Zlatan Ibrahimovic	48	120	2001-present	Ajax, Juventus, Inter Milan, Barcelona, AC Milan, PSG
9= Thomas Muller	48	124	2008-present	Bayern Munich
12= Eusebio	46	65	1961-74	Benfica
12= Filippo Inzaghi	46	81	1997-2012	Juventus, AC Milan
14 Didier Drogba	44	92	2003-15	Marseille, Chelsea, Galatasaray
15 Alessandro Del Piero	42	89	1995-2009	Juventus
16= Neymar	41	69	2013-present	Barcelona, PSG
16= Sergio Aguero	41	78	2008-present	Atletico Madrid, Man. City
18 Ferenc Puskas	36	41	1956-1966	Honved, Real Madrid
19 Edinson Cavani	35	65	2011-present	Napoli, PSG, Man United
20 Gerd Muller	34	35	1969-1977	Bayern Munich

RONALDO v MESSI

Cristiano Ronaldo may be 14 goals clear of Lionel Messi at the top of the charts but it's actually the little Argentinian who has the better strike rate, as he's played 27 fewer games in the UCL!

RONALDO
ONE UCL GOAL EVERY 1.31 GAMES

MESSI
ONE UCL GOAL EVERY 1.24 GAMES

ROO'S THE MAN

Wayne Rooney is the top-scoring English player in Champions League history. Wazza netted 30 times for Man. United between 2004 and 2015, including a hat-trick on his UCL debut against Fenerbahce. Wazza's ex-United team-mate Paul Scholes is second on the list with 24!

CHAMPIONS LEAGUE

REAL MADRID!

Real Madrid are the kings of the Champions League, having won the competition a record 13 times and reaching a record 16 finals. Check out some of their other records...

MOST MATCHES PLAYED

1 Real Madrid, 451 matches
2 Bayern Munich, 362 matches
3 Barcelona, 327 matches

MOST WINS

1 Real Madrid, 268 wins
2 Bayern Munich, 214 wins
3 Barcelona, 193 wins

MOST GOALS SCORED

1 Real Madrid, 992 goals
2 Bayern Munich, 751 goals
3 Barcelona, 653 goals

MOST FINALS REACHED

1 Real Madrid, 16 finals
2 Bayern Munich, 11 finals
2 AC Milan, 11 finals

Real Madrid and Spain legend Francisco Gento is the only player to win the tournament six times. His victories with Real came between 1956 and 1966!

Real also hold the record for the biggest win in a final – that was when they thumped Eintracht Frankfurt 7-3 in 1960!

THE BIGGEST WINS IN UCL HISTORY

REAL MADRID 8-0 SEVILLA
Quarter-final, 1957-58

LIVERPOOL 8-0 BESIKTAS
Group stage, 2007-08

REAL MADRID 8-0 MALMO
Group stage, 2015-16

TOP TRIVIA

TOP 10 CHAMPIONS LEAGUE APPEARANCES OF ALL TIME

PLAYER	GAMES	YEARS	CLUB(S)
1 Iker Casillas	177	1999-2019	Real Madrid, Porto
2 Cristiano Ronaldo	176	2003-present	Man. United, Real Madrid, Juventus
3 Xavi	151	1998-2015	Barcelona
4 Lionel Messi	149	2004-present	Barcelona
5 Raul	142	1995-2011	Real Madrid, Schalke
6 Ryan Giggs	141	1993-2014	Man. United
7= Andres Iniesta	130	2002-2018	Barcelona
7= Karim Benzema	130	2005-present	Lyon, Real Madrid
9 Sergio Ramos	129	2005-present	Real Madrid
10 Clarence Seedorf	125	1994-2012	Ajax, Real Madrid, AC Milan

CLEAN SHEET KING

Iker Casillas also holds the record for the most clean sheets in the competition. The Spanish shot-stopper recorded a huge 57 shut-outs in his UCL career – 50 with Real Madrid and another seven with Porto!

MOST GOALS IN A SEASON

45

Barcelona scored 45 goals in just 16 matches in 1999-2000 before losing to Valencia in the semi-final – Brazilian Rivaldo was their top scorer with ten!

MOST GOALS PER GAME

However, the most prolific team in UCL history was the Bayern Munich side of 2019-20, who hit 43 goals in just 11 games. That's an average of 3.91 per game, which is a UCL record!

CHAMPIONS LEAGUE

RELENTLESS RONALDO!

Cristiano Ronaldo was the top scorer for SIX consecutive seasons between 2013 and 2018 – and he'd already previously top-scored in 2007-08! CR7 is also the only player to score THREE hat-tricks in a single UCL season, achieving the feat in 2015-16!

MOST GOALS SCORED IN UCL CAMPAIGN

PLAYER	SEASON	GOALS
1 Cristiano Ronaldo	2013-14	17
2 Cristiano Ronaldo	2015-16	16
3= Cristiano Ronaldo	2017-18	15
3= Robert Lewandowski	2019-20	15
5= Jose Altafini	1962-63	14
5= Lionel Messi	2011-12	14

SEEDORF'S HAT-TRICK

Holland midfield legend Clarence Seedorf is the only player to have won the Champions League with THREE different clubs!

Ajax, 1994-95
Real Madrid, 1997-98
AC Milan, 2002-03 & 2006-07

TOP FIVE ASSISTERS IN THE UCL

PLAYER	ASSISTS	YEARS	CLUB(S)
1 Cristiano Ronaldo	42	2003-present	Man. United, R. Madrid, Juventus
2 Lionel Messi	36	2004-present	Barcelona
3 Angel Di Maria	32	2007-present	Benfica, Real Madrid, PSG
4 Ryan Giggs	31	1993-2014	Man. United
5 Xavi	30	1998-2015	Barcelona

DID YOU KNOW? The most assists in a single season is nine – and, surprisingly, it wasn't Cristiano Ronaldo, Zinedine Zidane or Ryan Giggs. No, it was Liverpool midfielder James Milner in 2017-18!

TOP TRIVIA

FIVE GUYS

Only two players in history have scored FIVE goals in a Champions League game!

LIONEL MESSI
Barcelona 7-1 Bayer Leverkusen (2011-12)

LUIZ ADRIANO
Shakhtar Donetsk 7-0 BATE (2014-15)

RAPID ROY

The fastest Champions League goal ever was scored by Dutch striker Roy Makaay in 2007. He netted for Bayern Munich against Real Madrid after just 10.12 seconds!

ZLAT'S MY BOY

Zlatan Ibrahimovic is the only player to have scored for SIX different teams in the Champions League – Ajax, Juventus, Inter Milan, Barcelona, AC Milan and PSG!

YOUNG GUN

Borussia Dortmund striker Youssoufa Moukoko became the youngest player in UCL history in December 2020 when, aged just 16 years and 18 days old, he made his debut against Zenit Saint Petersburg!

GOLDEN OLDIE

Italian keeper Marco Ballotta became the oldest player in UCL history when he played for Lazio against Real Madrid in 2007 – he was 43 years and 252 days!

MOST GAMES MANAGED IN THE UCL

1 ALEX FERGUSON
Matches 190 **Years** 1993-2013
Clubs Man. United

2 ARSENE WENGER
Matches 178 **Years** 1994-2017
Clubs Monaco, Arsenal

3 CARLO ANCELOTTI
Matches 166 **Years** 1997-present
Clubs Parma, Juventus, AC Milan, Chelsea, PSG, Real Madrid, Bayern Munich, Napoli

4 JOSE MOURINHO
Matches 151 **Years** 2002-present
Clubs Porto, Chelsea, Inter Milan, Real Madrid, Man. United, Tottenham

5 PEP GUARDIOLA
Matches 136 **Years** 2008-present
Clubs Barcelona, Bayern Munich, Man. City

LONDON CALLING

London has hosted the final seven times – that's more than any other city!

THE MAD WORLD OF

Back in 1893, Aston Villa smashed the world transfer record when they splashed out over £100 to sign Scottish striker Willie Groves from West Brom. Since then, the record has been broken 47 times.

WILLIE GROVES!

It's time to dive into the crazy world of record-breaking transfers!

TRANSFERS

TOP 10 MOST EXPENSIVE PLAYERS EVER

PLAYER	FROM	TO	FEE	YEAR
1 Neymar	Barcelona	PSG	£198m	2017
2 Kylian Mbappe	Monaco	PSG	£165m	2018
3 Eden Hazard	Chelsea	Real Madrid	£150m	2019
4 Philippe Coutinho	Liverpool	Barcelona	£142m	2018
5 Ousmane Dembele	B. Dortmund	Barcelona	£135m	2017
6 Joao Felix	Benfica	A. Madrid	£114m	2019
7 Antoine Griezmann	A. Madrid	Barcelona	£107m	2019
8 Paul Pogba	Juventus	Man. United	£89m	2016
9 Cristiano Ronaldo	Real Madrid	Juventus	£88m	2018
10 Gareth Bale	Tottenham	Real Madrid	£86m	2013

*Transfer fees include potential add-ons

PSG paid a world record £198 million when they signed Neymar in 2017.

THE MAD WORLD OF

THE MOST EXPENSIVE LINE-UP EVER

We've picked the most expensive player in each position to give us a line-up that cost more than ONE BILLION POUNDS!

Kepa Arrizabalaga
Athletic Bilbao
to Chelsea
£71.6m

Joao Cancelo
Juventus
to Man. City
£60m

Harry Maguire
Leicester to
Man. United
£80m

Virgil van Dijk
Southampton
to Liverpool
£75m

Lucas Hernandez
A. Madrid to
Bayern Munich
£68m

Paul Pogba
Juventus
to Man. Utd
£89m

Arthur
Barcelona
to Juventus
£66m

Philippe Coutinho
Liverpool to
Barcelona
£142m

Neymar
Barcelona
to PSG
£198m

Eden Hazard
Chelsea to
Real Madrid
£150m

Kylian Mbappe
Monaco
to PSG
£165m

DID YOU KNOW?
The last Englishman to be the world's most expensive player was Alan Shearer, when he moved from Blackburn to Newcastle for £15m in the summer of 1996!

TRANSFERS

DID YOU KNOW?

South American football legends Diego Maradona (Argentina) and Ronaldo (Brazil) are the only two players in history to have broken the world transfer record twice!

DIEGO MARADONA
1982 Boca Juniors to Barcelona £5m
1984 Barcelona to Napoli £6.9m

RONALDO
1996 PSV to Barcelona £13.2m
1997 Barcelona to Inter Milan £19.5m

MBAPPE'S TRANSFER HAT-TRICK

Kylian Mbappe smashed THREE transfer records when he moved from Monaco to PSG in 2018. He became the most expensive European footballer of all time, the most expensive teenager and the most expensive player to move within the same league!

SELECTED NATIONS' MOST EXPENSIVE EVER PLAYER

SCOTLAND **KIERAN TIERNEY**
Celtic to Arsenal £25m 2019

GERMANY **KAI HAVERTZ**
B. Leverkusen to Chelsea £70m 2020

SPAIN **KEPA ARRIZABALAGA**
Athletic Bilbao to Chelsea £71.6m 2018

ARGENTINA **GONZALO HIGUAIN**
Napoli to Juventus £75.3m 2016

SWEDEN **ZLATAN IBRAHIMOVIC**
Inter Milan to Barcelona £56m 2009

ITALY **JORGINHO**
Napoli to Chelsea £50m 2018

PORTUGAL **JOAO FELIX**
Benfica to Atletico Madrid £114m 2019

URUGUAY **LUIS SUAREZ**
Liverpool to Barcelona £65m 2014

CROATIA **MATEO KOVACIC**
Real Madrid to Chelsea £40.5m 2019

NIGERIA **VICTOR OSIMHEN**
Lille to Napoli £65m 2020

GHANA **THOMAS PARTEY**
Atletico Madrid to Arsenal £45m 2020

SENEGAL **SADIO MANE**
Southampton to Liverpool £34m 2016

USA **CHRISTIAN PULISIC**
B. Dortmund to Chelsea £58.3m 2019

COLOMBIA **JAMES RODRIGUEZ**
Monaco to Real Madrid £71m 2014

MEXICO **HIRVING LOZANO**
PSV to Napoli £36m 2019

TOP 5 BIGGEST PREMIER LEAGUE SIGNINGS

1 PAUL POGBA
Juventus to Man. United
£89m 2016

2 HARRY MAGUIRE
Leicester to Man. United
£80m 2019

3= ROMELU LUKAKU
Everton to Man. United
£75m 2017

4= VIRGIL VAN DIJK
Southampton to Liverpool
£75m 2018

5 NICOLAS PEPE
Lille to Arsenal
£72m 2019

ICONS OF THE

Football is all about heroes, superstars and legends – those players who can win a game by themselves, who can lead a team to glory and who write their names large in the history books. Right now, we're lucky enough to be witnessing two of the greatest of all time in Lionel Messi and Cristiano Ronaldo – but who else has been a certified icon of the game?

GAME

THE BEST PLAYER FROM EACH DECADE

1920s
RICARDO ZAMORA
SPAIN

1930s
GIUSEPPE MEAZZA
ITALY

1940s
STANLEY MATTHEWS
ENGLAND

1950s
ALFREDO DI STEFANO
ARGENTINA, SPAIN

1960s
PELE
BRAZIL

1970s
JOHAN CRUYFF
HOLLAND

1980s
DIEGO MARADONA
ARGENTINA

1990s
RONALDO
BRAZIL

2000s
ZINEDINE ZIDANE
FRANCE

2010s
LIONEL MESSI
ARGENTINA

WHO'S WON THE BALLON

THE WHAT? The Ballon d'Or! **WHAT'S THAT?** Well, Ballon d'Or is French for Golden Ball, and it's an annual football award presented by French magazine France Football. It's generally regarded as the most prestigious individual award for footballers!

PLAYER	WINS	YEARS
1 Lionel Messi	**6**	**2009, 2010, 2011, 2012, 2015, 2019**
2 Cristiano Ronaldo	5	2008, 2013, 2014, 2016, 2017
3= Michel Platini	**3**	**1983, 1984, 1985**
3= Johan Cruyff	3	1971, 1973, 1974
3= Marco van Basten	**3**	**1988, 1989, 1992**
6= Franz Beckenbauer	2	1972, 1976
6= Ronaldo	**2**	**1997, 2002**
6 =Alfredo Di Stefano	2	1957, 1959
6= Kevin Keegan	**2**	**1978, 1979**
6= Karl-Heinz Rummenigge	2	1980, 1981

D'OR THE MOST TIMES?

5 BALLON D'OR FACTS THAT WILL MAKE YOU GO "OH!"

Cristiano Ronaldo became the third United player to win it after Denis Law in 1964 and Bobby Charlton in 1966!

STAN THE MAN

Legendary England winger Stanley Matthews won the first Ballon d'Or in 1956. He played for Blackpool at the time!

THE No.1 No.1

Russian great Lev Yashin is the only keeper to ever win the award – he won it in 1963 while playing for Dynamo Moscow!

ENGLISH SUCCESS

The last English player to win the award was Liverpool striker Michael Owen in 2001. That year he scored 24 goals as the Reds won the FA Cup, EFL Cup, UEFA Cup and finished third in the Prem!

LA LIGA LEGENDS

The past 11 Ballon d'Or winners have all been from Barcelona or Real Madrid. The last one who wasn't was Cristiano Ronaldo in 2008, who was at Man. United!

THE BALLON D'OR DREAM TEAM

In 2020, France Football named its all-time all-star team after an internet poll and a final selection from their own team of global footy experts!

Lev Yashin
Soviet Union

Cafu
Brazil

Franz Beckenbauer
Germany

Paolo Maldini
Italy

Xavi
Spain

Lothar Matthaus
Germany

Diego Maradona
Argentina

Pele
Brazil

Cristiano Ronaldo
Portugal

Lionel Messi
Argentina

Ronaldo
Brazil

FOOTBALL ICONS

LIONEL MESSI

The unstoppable, record-breaking Barcelona GOAT!

Full name Lionel Andres Messi
Date of birth 24 June 1987
Place of birth Rosario, Argentina
Height 1.70m (5ft 7in)
Strongest foot left

CLUB CAREER

YEARS	CLUB	GAMES	GOALS
2004-present	Barcelona	778	672

INTERNATIONAL CAREER

YEARS	COUNTRY	GAMES	GOALS
2005-present	Argentina	142	71

PLAYING STYLE

An explosive dribbler, a pinpoint passer and a clinical finisher – this baller is a footballing phenomenon!

CAREER HIGHLIGHT

Scoring a ridiculous 91 goals in 2012, smashing the previous record of 85, held by Gerd Muller. He bagged 79 for Barcelona and another 12 for Argentina!

TROPHY CABINET

10 x La Liga **4 x** Champions League
6 x Ballon d'Or **13 x** Golden Boot (7x La Liga and 6x UCL) **6 x** European Golden Shoe
6 x La Liga Player of the Year

DID YOU KNOW?

In 2021, Messi became the first player to score 20 goals or more in 13 consecutive seasons in the top five European leagues!

CRISTIANO RONALDO

Prolific big-game goal machine!

FACT FILE

Full name Cristiano Ronaldo Dos Santos Aveiro **Date of birth** 5 February 1985 **Place of birth** Funchal, Portugal **Height** 1.87m (6ft 2in)
Strongest foot right

CLUB CAREER

YEARS	CLUB	GAMES	GOALS
2002-03	Sporting Lisbon	31	5
2003-09	Man. United	292	118
2009-18	Real Madrid	438	450
2018-present	Juventus	133	101

INTERNATIONAL CAREER

YEARS	COUNTRY	GAMES	GOALS
2003-present	Portugal	173	103

PLAYING STYLE

Once a winger, now a striker who brings power, control, precision and goals!

CAREER HIGHLIGHT

In 2017 CR7 won La Liga, the Champions League, the Ballon d'Or, the Spanish Super Cup, the UEFA Super Cup, the FIFA Club World Cup and was UCL top scorer!

TROPHY CABINET

7 x League titles (3 x Premier League, 2 x La Liga and 2 x Serie A) **5 x** Champions League **5 x** Ballon d'Or **12 x** Golden Boot (1 x Premier League, 3 x La Liga, 1 x Seria A, 7 x UCL) **4 x** European Golden Shoe **5 x** Player of the Year (2 x Premier League, 1 x La Liga and 2 x Serie A) **1 x** Euro 2016 **1 x** Nations League

DID YOU KNOW?

His five Ballon d'Or awards and four European Golden Shoe victories are both records for a European player!

FOOTBALL ICONS

DIEGO MARADONA

Devastating dribbler and match-winning maverick genius!

FACT FILE

Full name Diego Armando Maradona **Date of birth** 30 October 1960 **Place of birth** Lanus, Argentina **Date of death** 25 November 2020 (aged 60) **Height** 1.65m (5ft 5in) **Strongest foot** Left

CLUB CAREER

YEARS	CLUB	GAMES	GOALS
1976-81	Argentinos Juniors	166	116
1981-82	Boca Juniors	40	28
1982-84	Barcelona	58	38
1984-91	Napoli	259	115
1992-93	Sevilla	29	8
1993-94	Newell's Old Boys	5	0
1995-97	Boca Juniors	31	7

INTERNATIONAL CAREER

YEARS	COUNTRY	GAMES	GOALS
1977-1994	Argentina	91	34

PLAYING STYLE

A classic No.10, known for his dribbling, vision, ball control and creativity!

CAREER HIGHLIGHT

Captaining Argentina to victory in the 1986 World Cup – scoring five goals and producing the greatest individual display ever seen in the tournament's history!

TROPHY CABINET

3 x league titles (1 x Argentina, 2 x Serie A) **1 x** UEFA Cup **1 x** Serie A Golden Boot **1 x** World Cup **1 x** World Cup Golden Ball (best player) **1 x** FIFA Player of the Century

DID YOU KNOW?

He was the first player to break the world transfer record twice – when he moved to Barcelona for £5m, then to Napoli for £6.9m!

PELE

Football's first true global superstar who changed the game!

FACT FILE

Full name Edson Arantes Do Nascimento **Date of birth** 23 October 1940 **Place of birth** Tres Coracoes, Brazil **Height** 1.73m (5ft 8in) **Strongest foot** Right

CLUB CAREER

YEARS	CLUB	GAMES	GOALS
1956-74	Santos	656	643
1975-77	New York Cosmos	107	64

INTERNATIONAL CAREER

YEARS	COUNTRY	GAMES	GOALS
1957-71	Brazil	92	77

PLAYING STYLE

A powerful, skilful, all-round forward who could play as a striker or slightly deeper as a No.10 – he scored loads of goals and bagged tons of assists!

CAREER HIGHLIGHT

In the 1970 World Cup final, Pele scored the opening goal and set up two more as Brazil beat Italy 4-1. It was a record third World Cup win for Pele!

TROPHY CABINET

6 x Brazilian league, **10 x** Brazilian state league, **2 x** Copa Libertadores, **3 x** Brazilian league top scorer, **11 x** Brazilian state top scorer, **3 x** World Cup, **1 x** World Cup Golden Ball (best player) **1 x** FIFA Player of the Century

DID YOU KNOW?

It's been claimed that Pele scored a staggering 92 hat-tricks in his incredible 21-year career!

WOMEN'S FOOTBALL

DARE TO SHINE™

It's almost 130 years since the first women's match in the UK and three decades since the first Women's World Cup – but it's only in the last few years the game has truly gone global!

■ It's now played professionally in loads of countries all over the world, and 176 national teams compete internationally. Leagues have struck huge TV deals to broadcast matches to millions of viewers, and over 1.12 billion people worldwide watched the 2019 Women's World Cup in France!

A LITTLE HISTORY LESSON

Dick, Kerr Ladies FC, from Preston, was England's most famous – and best – women's team. Between 1917 and 1965 they played 833 games, winning 759, drawing 46 and losing just 28. During the early years, they attracted crowds from 4,000 up to 50,000. The star of Dick, Kerr Ladies was Lily Parr, a forward who reportedly scored more than 900 goals for the club!

THE LIONESSES!

ENGLAND FACT FILE

Head coach Sarina Wiegman **Captain** Steph Houghton **Home stadium** Various **First match** Scotland 2-3 England, 1972 **Biggest win** Hungary 0-13 England, 2005

MOST CAPPED PLAYER

PLAYER	CAPS	YEARS
1 Fara Williams	172	2001-21
2 Jill Scott	151	2006-present
3 Karen Carney	144	2005-19
4 Alex Scott	140	2004-17
5 Casey Stoney	130	2000-18

TOP GOALSCORERS

PLAYER	GOALS	YEARS
1 Kelly Smith	46	1995-2015
2 Kerry Davis	44	1982-98
3= Karen Walker	40	1988–2003
3= Fara Williams	40	2001-21
5 Ellen White	39	2010-present

ENGLAND ICONS

KELLY SMITH

England's all-time record scorer was a natural finisher who played for several teams in the USA before returning to Arsenal and hitting 73 goals in 66 games!

ALEX SCOTT

STEPH HOUGHTON

FAYE WHITE

FARA WILLIAMS

CURRENT STAR PLAYER

LUCY BRONZE

The left-back has won three UCL titles, English and French leagues, loads of domestic cups and the PFA Player of the Year twice!

WORLD CUP

APPEARANCES 5
BEST RESULT Third place, 2015

THE WSL

FACT FILE

Full name Football Association Women's Super League (FA WSL)
Founded 22 March 2010, 11 years ago **First season** 2011 **Country** England
Number of clubs 12 **Website** womenscompetitions.thefa.com

PAST WINNERS

YEAR	CHAMPIONS	RUNNERS-UP	TOP SCORER	GOALS
2011	Arsenal	Birmingham	Rachel Williams, Birmingham	14
2012	Arsenal	Birmingham	Kim Little, Arsenal	11
2013	Liverpool	Bristol City	Natasha Dowie, Liverpool	13
2014	Liverpool	Chelsea	Karen Carney, Birmingham	8
2015	Chelsea	Man. City	Beth Mead, Sunderland	12
2016	Man. City	Chelsea	Eniola Aluko, Chelsea	9
2017–18	Chelsea	Man. City	Ellen White, Birmingham	15
2018–19	Arsenal	Man. City	Vivianne Miedema, Arsenal	22
2019–20	Chelsea	Man. City	Vivianne Miedema, Arsenal	16
2020–21	Chelsea	Man. City	Sam Kerr, Chelsea	21

STRONG START Arsenal's Faye White was the first captain to lift the WSL trophy after the Gunners title win in 2011. They retained the crown the following season!

MOST APPEARANCES

160

JILL SCOTT Everton & Man. City

MOST GOALS

60

VIVIANNE MIEDEMA
Arsenal

MOST WSL TITLES

4

Chelsea 2015, 2017-18, 2019-20, 2020-21

MOST PLAYER OF THE SEASON AWARDS

2

LUCY BRONZE 2013-14 & 2016-17

FRAN KIRBY 2017-18 & 2020-21

THE WSL

BIGGEST WIN

11-1

Arsenal 11-1 Bristol City
2019–20

HIGHEST ATTENDANCE

38,262

Tottenham 0-2 Arsenal Tottenham Hotspur Stadium, 2019-20

WSL SUPERCLUB

CHELSEA

Full name Chelsea Football Club Women **Founded** 1992 (29 years ago) **Stadium** Kingsmeadow **Capacity** 4,850 **Manager** Emma Hayes **Star players** Sam Kerr, Pernille Harder, Fran Kirby

WSL SUPERCLUB

ARSENAL

Full name Arsenal Women Football Club **Founded** 1987 (34 years ago) **Stadium** Meadow Park **Capacity** 4,502 **Star players** Vivianne Miedema, Kim Little, Danielle van de Donk

WSL SUPERCLUB

MAN. CITY

Full name Man. City Women's Football Club **Founded** 1988 (32 years ago) **Stadium** Academy Stadium **Capacity** 7,000 **Manager** Gareth Taylor **Star players** Lucy Bronze, Ellen White, Steph Houghton

THE GLOBAL GAME

WOMEN'S CHAMPIONS LEAGUE

Full name UEFA Women's Champions League **Founded** 2001 **Region** Europe (UEFA) **No. of teams** 41 **Website** uefa.com/womenschampionsleague

MOST SUCCESSFUL CLUBS

CLUB	COUNTRY	WINS	YEARS WON
1 Lyon	France	7	2011, 2012, 2016, 2017, 2018, 2019, 2020
2 Frankfurt	Germany	4	2002, 2006, 2008, 2015
3= Umea	Sweden	2	2003, 2004
3= Wolfsburg	Germany	2	2013, 2014
3= Turbine Potsdam	Germany	2	2005, 2010
6= Arsenal	England	1	2007
6= Duisburg	Germany	1	2009
6= Barcelona	Spain	1	2021

Lyon have won the WCL a record seven times!

Lyon's Ada Hegerberg tops the WCL scoring charts!

TOP SCORERS

PLAYER	GOALS	CLUBS	YEARS
1 Ada Hegerberg	53	Stabaek, Turbine Potsdam, Lyon	2012-present
2 Anja Mittag	51	Turbine Potsdam, Rosengard, PSG, Wolfsburg	2004-19
3 Conny Pohlers	48	Turbine Potsdam, Frankfurt, Wolfsburg	2004-14
4 Eugenie Le Sommer	47	Lyon	2010-present
5 Marta	46	Umea, Tyreso, Rosengard	2005-present

WOMEN'S WORLD CUP

Full name FIFA Women's World Cup **Founded** 1991
Current champions USA **No. of teams** 32 (from 2023)
Website fifa.com/womensworldcup

MOST SUCCESSFUL NATIONS

COUNTRY	WINS	YEARS WON
1 USA	4	1991, 1999, 2015, 2019
2 Germany	2	2003, 2007
3= Norway	1	1995
3= Japan	1	2011

MOST WORLD CUP GOALS

17

MARTA
Brazil
2003-present

MOST INTERNATIONAL GOALS

NAME	COUNTRY	GOALS	YEARS
1 Christine Sinclair	Canada	186	2000–present
2 Abby Wambach	USA	184	2001-2015
3 Mia Hamm	USA	158	1987-2004
4 Kristine Lilly	USA	130	1987-2010
5 Birgit Prinz	Germany	128	1994-2011

MOST INTERNATIONAL CAPS

NAME	COUNTRY	CAPS	YEARS
1 Kristine Lilly	USA	354	1987-2010
2 Christie Pearce	USA	311	1997-2015
3 Carli Lloyd	USA	301	2005–present
4 Christine Sinclair	Canada	297	2000–present
5 Mia Hamm	USA	276	1987-2004

HOME NATIONS TOP SCORERS

NAME	COUNTRY	GOALS	YEARS
Rachel Furness	N. Ireland	31	2005–present
Julie Fleeting	Scotland	116	1996-2015
Helen Ward	Wales	42	2008–present

HOME NATIONS MOST CAPPED

NAME	COUNTRY	CAPS	YEARS
Julie Nelson	N. Ireland	114	2004–present
Gemma Fay	Scotland	203	1998-2017
Jess Fishlock	Wales	120	2006–present

INTERNATIONAL

In 1872, England and Scotland met in Glasgow for football's first-ever international. A crowd of 4,000 turned up to watch the drab 0-0 draw.

■ Today, 149 years after that game, there are 211 national football teams from all over the world, from Albania to Zimbabwe.

Since 1904, the global game has been governed by FIFA. International footy is divided into six regional confederations: Africa, Asia, Europe, North & Central America and the Caribbean, Oceania, and South America.

Countries from these confederations go head-to-head in friendlies and they also compete in their own continental competitions, such as the European Championship and the Copa America. However, easily the biggest of these competitions, overseen by FIFA, is of course the World Cup, which brings the world's best teams together for a month-long festival of football!

FOOTBALL

The current president of FIFA is Gianni Infantino, who has held the position since 2016!

Illustrations of the very first international match, which finished Scotland 0-0 England!

This is the Jules Rimet trophy – the original World Cup trophy given to the winner between 1930 and 1970!

FIFA

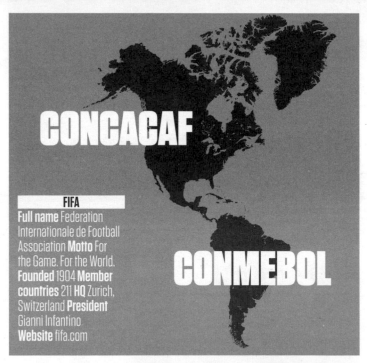

CONCACAF

CONMEBOL

FIFA

Full name Federation Internationale de Football Association **Motto** For the Game. For the World. **Founded** 1904 **Member countries** 211 **HQ** Zurich, Switzerland **President** Gianni Infantino **Website** fifa.com

UEFA

Full name Union of European Football Associations **Formed** 1954 **Region** Europe **Member countries** 55 **HQ** Nyon, Switzerland **President** Aleksander Ceferin **Website** uefa.com

AFC

Full name Asian Football Confederation **Formed** 1954 **Region** Asia **Member countries** 47 **HQ** Kuala Lumpur, Malaysia **President** Salman Bin Ibrahim Al-Khalifa **Website** the-afc.com

CAF

Full name Confederation of African Football **Formed** 1957 **Region** Africa **Member countries** 56 **HQ** Giza, Egypt **President** Patrice Motsepe **Website** cafonline.com

CONFEDERATIONS

OFC

Full name Oceania Football Confederation **Formed** 1966 **Region** Oceania (Australian continent) **Member countries** 13 **HQ** Auckland, New Zealand **President** Lambert Matlock **Website** oceaniafootball.com

CONCACAF

Full name Confederation of North, Central America and Caribbean Association Football **Formed** 1961 **Region** North America **Member countries** 41 **HQ** Florida, USA **President** Victor Montagliani **Website** concacaf.com

CONMEBOL

Full name South American Football Confederation **Formed** 1916 **Region** South America **Member countries** 10 **HQ** Gran Asuncion, Paraguay **President** Alejandro Dominguez **Website** conmebol.com

GLOBAL GOAL

TOP INTERNATIONAL SCORERS OF ALL TIME				
PLAYER	**COUNTRY**	**GOALS**	**GAMES**	**YEARS**
1 Ali Daei	**Iran**	**109**	**149**	**1993-2006**
2 Cristiano Ronaldo	Portugal	103	173	2003-present
3 Mokhtar Dahari	**Malaysia**	**89**	**142**	**1972-85**
4 Ferenc Puskas	Hungary	84	85	1945-56
5 Godfrey Chitalu	**Zambia**	**79**	**111**	**1968-80**
6 Hussein Saeed	Iraq	78	137	1977-90
7 Pele	**Brazil**	**77**	**92**	**1957-71**
8= Sandor Kocsis	Hungary	75	68	1948-56
8= Kunishige Kamamoto	**Japan**	**75**	**76**	**1964-77**
8= Bashar Abdullah	Kuwait	75	134	1996-2007

DEADLY DAEI

Ali Daei, a tall striker famed for his heading ability, spent five years in Germany playing for Bielefeld, Bayern Munich and Hertha Berlin. He went to the 1998 and 2006 World Cups with Iran – but he failed to bag on the big stage!

KINGS

TOP ACTIVE INTERNATIONAL SCORERS

PLAYER	COUNTRY	GOALS	GAMES	DEBUT
1 Cristiano Ronaldo	Portugal	103	173	2003
2 Sunil Chhetri	India	72	115	2005
3 Lionel Messi	Argentina	71	142	2005
4 Ali Mabkhout	UAE	68	87	2009
5 Robert Lewandowski	Poland	66	118	2008
6= Neymar	Brazil	64	103	2010
6= Luis Suarez	Uruguay	63	116	2007
8 Zlatan Ibrahimovic	Sweden	62	118	2001
9= Romelu Lukaku	Belgium	59	91	2010
9= Edin Dzeko	Bos. & Herz.	59	114	2007

CRISTIANO'S CHASE

Unsurprisingly, it's Cristiano Ronaldo who's closest to breaking Ali Daei's record. CR7's first ever international goal came 17 years ago at Euro 2004!

SUNIL CHHETRI

The 36-year-old Indian striker, second on the list, above, plays for Bengaluru FC in his homeland!

NATIONAL

THE MOST CAPPED 11 OF ALL-TIME

Mohamed Al-Deayea
Saudi Arabia
178 caps
1993-2006

Pavel Pardo
Mexico
146 caps
1996-2009

Sergio Ramos
Spain
180 caps
2005-present

Claudio Suarez
Mexico
177 caps
1992-2006

Maynor Figueroa
Honduras
165 caps
2003-present

Ahmed Hassan
Egypt
184 caps
1995-2012

Ahmed Mubarak
Oman
180 caps
2003-present

Vitalijs Astafjevs
Latvia
167 caps
1992-2010

Bader Al-Mutawa
Kuwait
181 caps
2003-present

Hossam Hassan
Egypt
176 caps
1985-2006

Cristiano Ronaldo
Portugal
173 caps
2003-present

HEROES

KING OF SPAIN
Real Madrid's Spanish star Sergio Ramos is the most-capped European player ever, with a massive 180 caps!

IVAN THE GREAT
Ecuador centre-back Ivan Hurtado is South America's most-capped player, clocking up 168 caps over a 22-year career!

AFRICAN ACE
Egyptian midfielder Ahmed Hassan, who played in Egypt, Turkey and Belgium in the 2000s, is the most-capped African player of all time!

THE WORLD CUP

The World Cup – or the FIFA World Cup, to give it its official name – is quite simply, the greatest sporting event on the entire planet.

■ It brings together 32 national teams from all over the world, who compete to be crowned World Cup winners.

The very first tournament was held in 1930, and apart from 1942 and 1946, which were cancelled due to World War II, it has been held every four years. The next World Cup, in Qatar in 2022, will be the 22nd.

The host nation automatically qualifies for the tournament, but the remaining teams all have to qualify from their respective continental zones.

Seventeen countries have hosted the World Cup, with five doing so twice. Eight countries have won it and only one nation has played in all 21 tournaments...

This football-loving South American nation are the undisputed kings of the World Cup!

This record-breaking German striker always saved his best for the World Cup finals!

The World Cup has created heroes, villains and tons of magical moments!

WORLD CUP

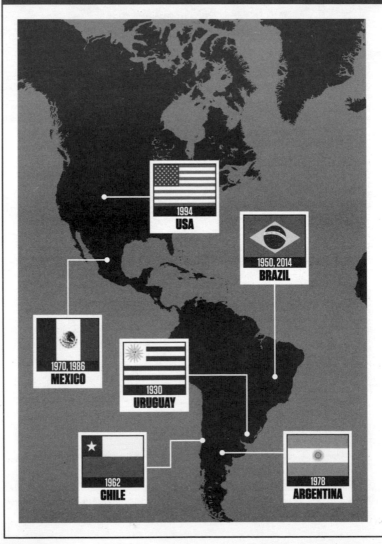

1994
USA

1950, 2014
BRAZIL

1970, 1986
MEXICO

1930
URUGUAY

1962
CHILE

1978
ARGENTINA

HOST NATIONS

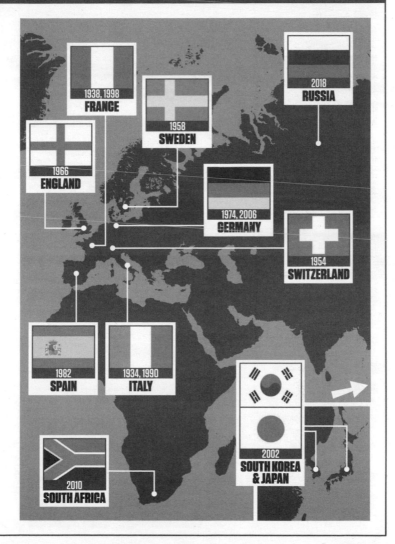

1938, 1998
FRANCE

1958
SWEDEN

2018
RUSSIA

1966
ENGLAND

1974, 2006
GERMANY

1954
SWITZERLAND

1982
SPAIN

1934, 1990
ITALY

2002
SOUTH KOREA & JAPAN

2010
SOUTH AFRICA

URUGUAY 1930

TOURNAMENT STATS

Teams **13**
Matches played **18**
Goals scored **70**
Average attendance
32,808 per match

FINAL POSITIONS

Winners **Uruguay**
Runners-up **Argentina**
Third place **United States**
Fourth place **Yugoslavia**

THE FINAL

URUGUAY	4-2	ARGENTINA

Dorado 12, Cea 57,
Iriarte 68, Castro 89

Peucelle 20,
Stabile 37

Date 30 July 1930 **Venue** Estadio Centenario, Montevideo
Referee Jean Langenus (Belgium) **Attendance** 68,346

CHAMPIONS URUGUAY

TOP SCORERS

1 **Guillermo Stabile** Argentina **8 goals**
2 **Pedro Cea** Uruguay **5 goals**
3 **Bert Patenaude** USA **4 goals**

GOLDEN BOOT
Guillermo Stabile
Argentina

GOLDEN BALL
Jose Nasazzi
Uruguay

ITALY 1934

TOURNAMENT STATS

Teams **16**
Matches played **17**
Goals scored **70**
Average attendance
21,353 per match

FINAL POSITIONS

Winners **Italy**
Runners-up **Czechoslovakia**
Third place **Germany**
Fourth place **Austria**

THE FINAL

ITALY	2-1 (AET)	CZECHOSLOVAKIA

Orsi 81,
Schiavio 95

Puc 71

Date 10 June 1934 **Venue** Stadio Nazionale PNF, Rome
Referee Ivan Eklind (Sweden) **Attendance** 55,000

CHAMPIONS ITALY

TOP SCORERS

1 **Oldrich Nejedly** Czechoslovakia **5 goals**
2= **Edmund Conen** Germany **4 goals**
2= **Angelo Schiavio** Italy **4 goals**

GOLDEN BOOT
Oldrich Nejedly
Czechoslovakia

GOLDEN BALL
Giuseppe Meazza
Italy

FRANCE 1938

TOURNAMENT STATS

Teams **15**
Matches played **18**
Goals scored **84**
Average attendance
20,824 per match

FINAL POSITIONS

Winners **Italy**
Runners-up **Hungary**
Third place **Brazil**
Fourth place **Sweden**

THE FINAL

ITALY	4-2	HUNGARY

Colaussi 6, 35,
Piola 16, 82

Titkos 8,
Sarosi 70

Date 19 June 1938 **Venue** Stade Olympique de Colombes, Paris
Referee Georges Capdeville (France) **Attendance** 45,000

CHAMPIONS ITALY

TOP SCORERS

1 **Leonidas** Brazil **7 goals**
2 **Gyorgy Sarosi** Hungary **5 goals**
3 **Gyula Zsengeller** Hungary **5 goals**
4 **Silvio Piola** Italy **5 goals**

GOLDEN BOOT
Leonidas
Brazil

GOLDEN BALL
Leonidas
Brazil

BRAZIL 1950

TOURNAMENT STATS

Teams **13**
Matches played **22**
Goals scored **88**
Average attendance
47,511 per match

FINAL POSITIONS

Winners **Uruguay**
Runners-up **Brazil**
Third place **Sweden**
Fourth place **Spain**

THE FINAL

URUGUAY	2-1	BRAZIL

Schiaffino 66,
Ghiggia 79

Friaca 47

Date 16 July 1950 **Venue** Estadio Do Maracana, Rio De Janeiro
Referee George Reader (England) **Attendance** 199,854

CHAMPIONS URUGUAY

TOP SCORERS

1 **Ademir** Brazil **8 goals** 2 **Oscar Miguez** Uruguay **5 goals**
3= **Chico** Brazil **4 goals** 3= **Estanislau Basora** Spain **4 goals**
3= **Telmo Zarra** Spain **4 goals** 3= **Alcides Ghiggia** Uruguay
4 goals

GOLDEN BOOT
Ademir
Brazil

GOLDEN BALL
Zizinho
Brazil

SWITZERLAND 1954

TOURNAMENT STATS
Teams **16**
Matches played **26**
Goals scored **140**
Average attendance
29,562 per match

FINAL POSITIONS
Winners **West Germany**
Runners-up **Hungary**
Third place **Austria**
Fourth place **Uruguay**

THE FINAL
WEST GERMANY 3-2 HUNGARY

Morlock 10,
Rahn 18, 84

Puskas 6,
Czibor 8

Date 4 July 1954 **Venue** Wankdorf Stadium, Bern
Referee William Ling (England) **Attendance** 62,500

CHAMPIONS WEST GERMANY

TOP SCORERS
1 **Sandor Kocsis** Hungary **11 goals**
2= **Erich Probst** Austria **6 goals**
2= **Josef Hugi** Switzerland **6 goals**
2= **Max Morlock** West Germany **6 goals**

GOLDEN BOOT
Sandor Kocsis
Hungary

GOLDEN BALL
Ferenc Puskas
Hungary

SWEDEN 1958

TOURNAMENT STATS
Teams **16**
Matches played **35**
Goals scored **126**
Average attendance
23,423 per match

FINAL POSITIONS
Winners **Brazil**
Runners-up **Sweden**
Third place **France**
Fourth place **West Germany**

THE FINAL
BRAZIL 5-2 SWEDEN

Vava 9, 32, Pele 55, 90,
Zagallo 68

Liedholm 4,
Simonsson 80

Date 29 June 1958 **Venue** Rasunda Stadium, Solna
Referee Maurice Guigue (France) **Attendance** 49,737

CHAMPIONS BRAZIL

TOP SCORERS
1 **Just Fontaine** France **13 goals**
2= **Pele** Brazil **6 goals**
2= **Helmut Rahn** West Germany **6 goals**

GOLDEN BOOT
Just Fontaine
France

GOLDEN BALL
Didi
Brazil

CHILE 1962

TOURNAMENT STATS

Teams **16**
Matches played **32**
Goals scored **89**
Average attendance
27,912 per match

FINAL POSITIONS

Winners **Brazil**
Runners-up **Czechoslovakia**
Third place **Chile**
Fourth place **Yugoslavia**

THE FINAL

BRAZIL **3-1** CZECHOSLOVAKIA

Amarildo 17, Zito 69,   Masopust 15
Vava 78

Date 17 June 1962 **Venue** Estadio Nacional, Santiago
Referee Nikolay Latyshev (Soviet Union) **Attendance** 68,679

CHAMPIONS BRAZIL

TOP SCORERS

1 **Garrincha** Brazil **4 goals**, 1= **Vava** Brazil **4 goals**,
1= **Leonel Sanchez** Chile **4 goals**, 1= **Florian Albert**
Hungary **4 goals**, 1= **Valentin Ivanov** Soviet Union
4 goals, 1= **Drazan Jerkovic** Yugoslavia **4 goals**

GOLDEN BOOT
**6 players on
4 goals**

GOLDEN BALL
Garrincha
Brazil

Brazil line up after beating Czechoslovakia in the Chilean capital Santiago in 1962!

ENGLAND 1966

TOURNAMENT STATS

Teams **16**
Matches played **32**
Goals scored **89**
Average attendance
48,848 per match

FINAL POSITIONS

Winners **England**
Runners-up **West Germany**
Third place **Portugal**
Fourth place **Soviet Union**

THE FINAL

ENGLAND **4-2** (AET) **WEST GERMANY**

Hurst 18, 101, 120,
Peters 78

Haller 12,
Weber 89

Date 30 July 1966 **Venue** Wembley Stadium, London
Referee Gottfried Dienst (Switzerland) **Attendance** 96,924

CHAMPIONS ENGLAND

TOP SCORERS

1 **Eusebio** Portugal **9 goals**, 2 **Helmut Haller** West Germany
6 goals, 3= **Geoff Hurst** England **4 goals**, 3= **Ferenc Bene**
Hungary **4 goals**, 3= **Valeriy Porkujan** Soviet Union **4 goals**
3= **Franz Beckenbauer** West Germany **4 goals**

GOLDEN BOOT
Eusebio
Portugal

GOLDEN BALL
Bobby Charlton
England

WEST GERMANY Manager: Helmut Schon

Tilkowski

Hoettges | Schulz | Weber | Schnellinger

Beckenbauer | Overath

Haller | Seeler | Held | Emerich

Hunt | Hurst

Peters | B. Charlton | Ball

Stiles

Wilson | Moore | J. Charlton | Cohen

Banks

ENGLAND Manager: Alf Ramsey

ENGLAND'S ROAD TO GLORY

Group 1 England 0-0 Uruguay
Group 1 England 2-0 Mexico
Group 1 England 2-0 France
Quarter-final England 1-0 Argentina
Semi-final England 2-1 Portugal
Final England 4-2 West Germany (AET)

Did it cross the line? Geoff Hurst gives England a 3-2 lead with the most controversial goal in World Cup history!

England celebrate after winning the 1966 World Cup at Wembley Stadium!

MEXICO 1970

TOURNAMENT STATS

Teams **16**
Matches played **32**
Goals scored **95**
Average attendance
50,127 per match

FINAL POSITIONS

Winners **Brazil**
Runners-up **Italy**
Third place **West Germany**
Fourth place **Uruguay**

THE FINAL

BRAZIL 4-1 ITALY

Pele 18, Gerson 66,   Boninsegna 37
Jairzinho 71, Carlos Alberto 86

Date 21 June 1970 **Venue** Estadio Azteca, Mexico City
Referee Rudi Glockner (East Germany) **Attendance** 107,412

CHAMPIONS BRAZIL

TOP SCORERS

1 **Gerd Muller** West Germany **10 goals**
2 **Jairzinho** Brazil **7 goals**
3 **Teofilo Cubillas** Peru **5 goals**

GOLDEN BOOT
Gerd Muller
West Germany

GOLDEN BALL
Pele
Brazil

WEST GERMANY 1974

TOURNAMENT STATS

Teams **16**
Matches played **38**
Goals scored **97**
Average attendance
49,099 per match

FINAL POSITIONS

Winners **West Germany**
Runners-up **Holland**
Third place **Poland**
Fourth place **Brazil**

THE FINAL

HOLLAND 1-2 WEST GERMANY

Neeskens 2 (pen)   Breitner 25 (pen),
                                                    Muller 43

Date 7 July 1974 **Venue** Olympiastadion, Munich
Referee Jack Taylor (England) **Attendance** 75,200

CHAMPIONS WEST GERMANY

TOP SCORERS

1 **Grzegorz Lato** Poland **7 goals**
2= **Johan Neeskens** Holland **5 goals**
2= **Andrzej Szarmach** Poland **5 goals**

GOLDEN BOOT
Grzegorz Lato
Poland

GOLDEN BALL
Johan Cruyff
Holland

ARGENTINA 1978

TOURNAMENT STATS

Teams **16**
Matches played **38**
Goals scored **102**
Average attendance
40,679 per match

FINAL POSITIONS

Winners **Argentina**
Runners-up **Holland**
Third place **Brazil**
Fourth place **Italy**

THE FINAL

ARGENTINA 3-1 (AET) HOLLAND

Kempes 38, 105,   Nanninga 82
Bertoni 115

Date **25 June 1978** Venue Estadio Monumental, Buenos Aires
Referee Sergio Gonella (Italy) Attendance 71,483

CHAMPIONS ARGENTINA

TOP SCORERS

1 **Mario Kempes** Argentina **6 goals**
2= **Rob Rensenbrink** Holland **5 goals**
2= **Teofilo Cubillas** Peru **5 goals**

GOLDEN BOOT	GOLDEN BALL
Mario Kempes	**Mario Kempes**
Argentina	Argentina

SPAIN 1982

TOURNAMENT STATS

Teams **24**
Matches played **52**
Goals scored **146**
Average attendance
40,572 per match

FINAL POSITIONS

Winners **Italy**
Runners-up **West Germany**
Third place **Poland**
Fourth place **France**

THE FINAL

ITALY 3-1 WEST GERMANY

Rossi 57, Tardelli 69,   Breitner 83
Altobelli 81

Date **11 July 1982** Venue Santiago Bernabeu, Madrid
Referee Arnaldo Cezar Coelho (Brazil) Attendance 90,000

CHAMPIONS ITALY

TOP SCORERS

1 **Paolo Rossi** Italy **6 goals**
2 **Karl-Heinz Rummenigge** West Germany **5 goals**
3= **Zico** Brazil **4 goals**, 3= **Zbigniew Boniek** Poland **4 goals**

GOLDEN BOOT	GOLDEN BALL
Paolo Rossi	**Paolo Rossi**
Italy	Italy

MEXICO 1986

TOURNAMENT STATS

Teams **24**
Matches played **52**
Goals scored **132**
Average attendance
46,039 per match

FINAL POSITIONS

Winners **Argentina**
Runners-up **West Germany**
Third place **France**
Fourth place **Belgium**

THE FINAL

ARGENTINA 3-2 WEST GERMANY

Brown 23, Valdano 56,   Rummenigge 74,
Burruchaga 84   Voller 81

Date 29 June 1986 **Venue** Estadio Azteca, Mexico City
Referee Romualdo Arppi Filho (Brazil) **Attendance** 114,600

CHAMPIONS ARGENTINA

TOP SCORERS

1 **Gary Lineker** England **6 goals** 2= **Diego Maradona**
Argentina **5 goals** 2= **Careca** Brazil **5 goals** 2= **Emilio**
Butragueno Spain **5 goals**

GOLDEN BOOT
Gary Lineker
England

GOLDEN BALL
Diego Maradona
Argentina

Argentina captain Diego Maradona was the standout star of the 1986 World Cup!

ITALY 1990

TOURNAMENT STATS

Teams **24**
Matches played **52**
Goals scored **115**
Average attendance
48,389 per match

FINAL POSITIONS

Winners **West Germany**
Runners-up **Argentina**
Third place **Italy**
Fourth place **England**

THE FINAL

WEST GERMANY 1-0 ARGENTINA

Brehme 85 (pen)

Date 8 July 1990 **Venue** Stadio Olimpico, Rome
Referee Edgardo Codesal Mendez (Mexico) **Attendance** 73,603

CHAMPIONS WEST GERMANY

TOP SCORERS

1 **Salvatore Schillaci** Italy 6 goals 2 **Tomas Skuhravy**
Czechoslovakia 5 goals 3= **Roger Milla** Cameroon 4 goals
3= **Gary Lineker** England 4 goals 3= **Michel** Spain 4 goals
3= **Lothar Matthaus** West Germany 4 goals

GOLDEN BOOT
Salvatore
Schillaci Italy

GOLDEN BALL
Salvatore
Schillaci Italy

West Germany got revenge after their final
defeat by Argentina four years earlier!

MEXICO 1970

WORLD CUP KING Pele celebrates a record third World Cup win after Brazil's thumping 4-1 victory over Italy in the final!

ARGENTINA 1978

SPAIN 1982

MASCOT MADNESS This is Gauchito, mascot for the 1978 World Cup, and Naranjito, an orange, who was mascot in 1982!

MEXICO 1986

AWESOME AZTECA In 1986, the iconic Azteca Stadium in Mexico became the first to host two World Cup finals, after already doing so in 1970!

MAGIC MARADONA The undisputed star of the 1986 tournament was Diego Maradona – his two goals for Argentina against England will never be forgotten!

ITALY 1990

UNLUCKY LIONS This is the England team that lost on penalties to West Germany in the 1990 World Cup semi-final!

THRILLER MILLA Cameroon and their 38-year-old striker Roger Milla were the surprise stars of Italia '90 as they reached the quarter-finals!

GAZZA MANIA Paul Gascoigne and his tears became legendary during England's run to the semi-finals!

USA 1994

TOURNAMENT STATS
Teams **24**
Matches played **52**
Goals scored **141**
Average attendance
69,174 per match

FINAL POSITIONS
Winners **Brazil**
Runners-up **Italy**
Third place **Sweden**
Fourth place **Bulgaria**

THE FINAL
BRAZIL **0-0** (AET) ITALY

Brazil won 3-2 on penalties

Date 17 July, 1994 **Venue** Rose Bowl, Pasadena
Referee Sandor Puhl (Hungary) **Attendance** 94,194

CHAMPIONS BRAZIL

TOP SCORERS
1= **Hristo Stoichkov** Bulgaria **6 goals** 1= **Oleg Salenko**
Russia **6 goals** 3= **Romario** Brazil **5 goals** 3= **Roberto**
Baggio Italy **5 goals** 3= **Jurgen Klinsmann** Germany **5**
goals 3= **Kennet Andersson** Sweden **5 goals**

GOLDEN BOOT
Hristo Stoichkov
Bulgaria & Oleg
Salenko Russia

GOLDEN BALL
Romario
Brazil

FRANCE 1998

TOURNAMENT STATS
Teams **32**
Matches played **64**
Goals scored **171**
Average attendance
43,511 per match

FINAL POSITIONS
Winners **France**
Runners-up **Brazil**
Third place **Croatia**
Fourth place **Holland**

THE FINAL
BRAZIL **0-3** FRANCE

Zidane 27, 45,
Petit 90

Date 12 July 1998 **Venue** Stade de France, Saint-Denis
Referee Said Belqola (Morocco) **Attendance** 80,000

CHAMPIONS FRANCE

TOP SCORERS
1 **Davor Suker** Croatia **6 goals**
2= **Gabriel Batistuta** Argentina **5 goals**
2= **Christian Vieri** Italy **5 goals**

GOLDEN BOOT
Davor Suker
Croatia

GOLDEN BALL
Ronaldo
Brazil

S. KOREA & JAPAN 2002

TOURNAMENT STATS
Teams **32**
Matches played **64**
Goals scored **161**
Average attendance
42,269 per match

FINAL POSITIONS
Winners **Brazil**
Runners-up **Germany**
Third place **Turkey**
Fourth place **South Korea**

TOP SCORERS
1 **Ronaldo** Brazil **8 goals**
2= **Rivaldo** Brazil **5 goals**
2= **Miroslav Klose** Germany **5 goals**

THE FINAL

GERMANY	0-2	BRAZIL

Ronaldo 67, 79

Date 30 June 2002 **Venue** International Stadium, Yokohama
Referee Pierluigi Collina (Italy) **Attendance** 69,029

CHAMPIONS BRAZIL

GOLDEN BOOT
Ronaldo
Brazil

GOLDEN BALL
Oliver Kahn
Germany

GERMANY 2006

TOURNAMENT STATS
Teams **32**
Matches played **64**
Goals scored **147**
Average attendance
52,491 per match

FINAL POSITIONS
Winners **Italy**
Runners-up **France**
Third place **Germany**
Fourth place **Portugal**

TOP SCORERS
1 **Miroslav Klose** Germany **5 goals**
2= **Eight players on 3 goals**

THE FINAL

ITALY	1-1 (AET)	FRANCE

Materazzi 19   Zidane 7 (pen)

Italy won 5-3 on penalties

Date 9 July 2006 **Venue** Olympiastadion, Berlin
Referee Horacio Elizondo (Argentina) **Attendance** 69,000

CHAMPIONS ITALY

GOLDEN BOOT
Miroslav Klose
Germany

GOLDEN BALL
Zinedine Zidane
France

USA 1994

PENALTY PAIN Roberto Baggio, who'd fired his Italian team to the final, suffers penalty shootout heartbreak when his miss from the spot hands the World Cup to Brazil!

FRANCE 1998

SUPER SUKER Croatian striker Davor Suker celebrates his semi-final goal against France on the way to winning the Golden Boot!

SOUTH KOREA & JAPAN 2002

PENALTY GAIN England skipper David Beckham smashes home a penalty to give England a 1-0 group stage win over Argentina – and revenge for World Cup defeats in 1986 and 1998!

GERMANY 2006

ZIZOU'S GOODBYE It's 1-1 in the 2006 final between Italy and France, when Zinedine Zidane headbutts Italian Marco Materrazi – he gets sent off and his team lose on pens!

RED FOR ROO Wayne Rooney is sent off for a stamp on Portugal defender Ricardo Carvalho in the quarter-finals, as England exit another World Cup on penalties!

SOUTH AFRICA 2010

TOURNAMENT STATS
Teams **32**
Matches played **64**
Goals scored **145**
Average attendance
49,670 per match

FINAL POSITIONS
Winners **Spain**
Runners-up **Holland**
Third place **Germany**
Fourth place **Uruguay**

THE FINAL

HOLLAND **0-1** (AET) **SPAIN**

Iniesta 115

Date 11 July 2010 **Venue** FNB Stadium, Johannesburg
Referee Howard Webb (England) **Attendance** 84,490

CHAMPIONS SPAIN

TOP SCORERS
1= **Thomas Muller** Germany **5 goals**
1= **Wesley Sneijder** Holland **5 goals**
1= **David Villa** Spain **5 goals**
1= **Diego Forlan** Uruguay **5 goals**

GOLDEN BOOT
**4 players
on 5 goals**

GOLDEN BALL
Diego Forlan
Uruguay

BRAZIL 2014

TOURNAMENT STATS
Teams **32**
Matches played **64**
Goals scored **171**
Average attendance
53,592 per match

FINAL POSITIONS
Winners **Germany**
Runners-up **Argentina**
Third place **Holland**
Fourth place **Brazil**

THE FINAL

GERMANY **1-0** (AET) **ARGENTINA**

Gotze 112

Date 13 July 2014 **Venue** Maracana, Rio de Janeiro
Referee Nicola Rizzoli (Italy) **Attendance** 74,738

CHAMPIONS GERMANY

TOP SCORERS
1 **James Rodriguez** Colombia **6 goals**
2 **Thomas Muller** Germany **5 goals** 3= **Lionel Messi**
Argentina **4 goals** 3= **Neymar** Brazil **4 goals**
3= **Robin van Persie** Holland **4 goals**

GOLDEN BOOT
James Rodriguez
Colombia

GOLDEN BALL
Lionel Messi
Argentina

RUSSIA 2018

TOURNAMENT STATS

Teams **32**
Matches played **64**
Goals scored **169**
Average attendance
47,371 per match

FINAL POSITIONS

Winners **France**
Runners-up **Croatia**
Third place **Belgium**
Fourth place **England**

THE FINAL

FRANCE 4-2 CROATIA

Mandzukic 18 (og), Griezmann
38 (pen), Pogba 59, Mbappe 65

Perisic 28,
Mandzukic 69

Date 15 July 2018 **Venue** Luzhniki Stadium, Moscow
Referee Nestor Pitana (Argentina) **Attendance** 78,011

CHAMPIONS FRANCE

TOP SCORERS

1 **Harry Kane** England **6 goals** 2= **Romelu Lukaku** Belgium
4 goals 2= **Antoine Griezmann** France **4 goals** 2= **Kylian
Mbappe** France **4 goals** 2= **Cristiano Ronaldo** Portugal
4 goals 2= **Denis Cheryshev** Russia **4 goals**

GOLDEN BOOT
Harry Kane
England

GOLDEN BALL
Luka Modric
Croatia

Kylian Mbappe celebrates after giving France a 4-1 lead in the 2018 final!

SOUTH AFRICA 2010

SPANISH STARS Sergio Ramos, final hero Andres Iniesta and Xabi Alonso celebrate Spain's first World Cup triumph!

WHAT A NOISE The 2010 World Cup was dominated off the pitch by the vuvuzela, a long horn blown by fans throughout the game. Some players even wanted it banned!

BRAZIL 2014

GERMAN GLORY Germany celebrate winning the World Cup for the fourth time, thanks to Mario Gotze's extra-time goal!

RUSSIA 2018

HITMAN HARRY Harry Kane nets a vital injury-time winner in England's first game of the World Cup – he goes on to score five more and claim the Golden Boot!

ALLEZ LES BLEUS Kylian Mbappe poses for photos with the World Cup after France's 4-2 final win over Croatia in Moscow's Luzhniki Stadium!

WORLD CUP TOP

These guys have scored more goals at World Cup tournaments than anyone else in the history of the game!

PLAYER	COUNTRY	GOALS	GAMES	TOURNAMENTS
1 Miroslav Klose	Germany	16	24	2002, 2006, 2010, 2014
2 Ronaldo	Brazil	15	19	1994, 1998, 2002, 2006
3 Gerd Muller	West Germany	14	13	1970, 1974
4 Just Fontaine	France	13	6	1958
5 Pele	Brazil	12	14	1958, 1962, 1966, 1970
6= Sandor Kocsis	Hungary	11	5	1954
6= Jurgen Klinsmann	W. Germany & Germany	11	17	1990, 1994, 1998
8= Helmut Rahn	West Germany	10	10	1954, 1958
8= Gary Lineker	England	10	12	1986, 1990
8= Gabriel Batistuta	Argentina	10	12	1994, 1998, 2002
8= Teofilo Cubillas	Peru	10	13	1970, 1978, 1982
8= Thomas Muller	Germany	10	16	2010, 2014, 2018
8= Grzegorz Lato	Poland	10	20	1974, 1978, 1982

WHO IS MIROSLAV KLOSE?

Here he is – the man who's scored more World Cup goals than anyone else in history! His first-half goal in Germany's 7-1 semi-final thrashing of Brazil at the 2014 World Cup was his 16th and last before retiring. Here are five things you might not know about Miroslav Josef Klose!

- He was born in Poland in 1978.
- He is Germany's all-time record goalscorer with 71 goals in 137 games.
- He played in the Bundesliga for Kaiserslautern, Werder Bremen and Bayern Munich before finishing his career with Italian club Lazio.
- He won the Golden Boot at the 2006 World Cup.
- Germany never lost a game when he scored.

SCORERS

RONALDO

Before Klose's two goals at the 2014 World Cup, Ronaldo was the tournament's top scorer. The Brazilian icon, who played for Barcelona, Real Madrid, Inter Milan and AC Milan, among others, fired his nation to glory at the 2002 World Cup, bagging the Golden Boot in the process!

GARY LINEKER

The 1986 Golden Boot winner is England's record goalscorer at World Cups. Lineker, a star in the 1980s and 90s for Leicester, Everton, Barcelona and Tottenham, is his country's third top scorer of all time!

JUST FONTAINE

The France striker, who was born in Morocco and made his name with Reims, still holds the record for the most goals in a single tournament. His 13 strikes came in just six games at the 1958 World Cup!

WORLD CUP

WORLD CUP GOAL KINGS!

Miroslav Klose and Brazilian Ronaldo may top the scoring charts at tournaments, but there are a couple of familiar faces (and one not so) when you factor in goals scored during World Cup qualifying, too!

MOST WORLD CUP GOALS (INCLUDING QUALIFYING)

1 **Carlos Ruiz** Guatemala **39 goals**
2 **Cristiano Ronaldo** Portugal **38 goals**
3 **Luis Suarez** Uruguay **32 goals**

Guatemala legend Carlos Ruiz, a striker who played in the MLS, Mexico, Paraguay and Greece as well as his homeland, never actually played at a World Cup – but between 1998 and 2016 he scored 39 goals in qualifiers!

HUNGARY FOR GOALS

Hungary's 10-1 group stage win over El Salvador at Spain '82 is the biggest win in the history of the tournament – amazingly, it was their only win!

The famous Hungary team of 1954 is also the most prolific in World Cup history. They scored a record 27 goals during their five game-run to the final before losing 3-2 to West Germany!

THE FASTEST GOAL

Turkish striker Hakan Sukur scored the quickest goal in the tournament's history when he netted after just 11 seconds of Turkey's 3-2 win over South Korea in the third-place play-off at the 2002 World Cup!

OLD MAN MILLA

Roger Milla became oldest goalscorer in World Cup history when, aged 42 years and 39 days old, he scored in Cameroon's 6-1 defeat by Russia at USA '94!

SALENKO STRIKES

In the same game, Russia striker Oleg Salenko broke the record for most goals scored in a World Cup match when he bagged FIVE of Russia's six goals!

TOP TRIVIA

BRILL BRAZIL!

The kings of the World Cup are the boys from Brazil. They have won the tournament a record five times and are the only country to play at EVERY World Cup finals. Check out some of their other records, too...

MOST WORLD CUP TOURNAMENTS

1 Brazil, 21 tournaments
2 Germany, 19 tournaments
3 Italy, 18 tournaments

MOST MATCHES PLAYED

1= Brazil, 109 matches
1= Germany, 109 matches
3 Italy, 83 matches

MOST WINS

1 Brazil, 73 wins
2 Germany, 67 wins
3 Italy, 45 wins

MOST GOALS SCORED

1 Brazil, 229 goals
2 Germany, 226 goals
3 Argentina, 137 goals

PELE'S HAT-TRICK

Brazil ledge Pele is the only player to win three World Cup winners' medals (in 1958, 1962 and 1970)!

Pele is also officially the World Cup's king of the assist – his six in 1970 is a tournament record, and his total of ten is more than any other player in the history of the tournament!

MOST WORLD CUP APPEARANCES

1 Lothar Matthaus Germany 25 games
2 Miroslav Klose Germany 24 games
3 Paolo Maldini Italy 23 games

CLEAN SHEETS SHILTS

No World Cup keeper has kept more clean sheets (ten) than England's Peter Shilton. He shares the record with French stopper Fabien Barthez!

WORLD CUP

BRAZIL
5 WINS 1958, 1962, 1970, 1994, 2002
PROFILE ON p115

URUGUAY
2 WINS 1930, 1950
PROFILE ON p122

ARGENTINA
2 WINS 1978, 1986
PROFILE ON p114

WINNERS

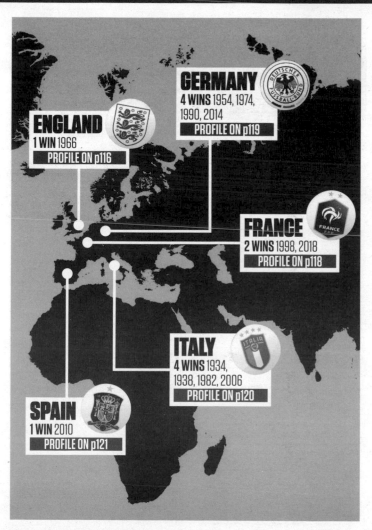

GERMANY
4 WINS 1954, 1974, 1990, 2014
PROFILE ON p119

ENGLAND
1 WIN 1966
PROFILE ON p116

FRANCE
2 WINS 1998, 2018
PROFILE ON p118

ITALY
4 WINS 1934, 1938, 1982, 2006
PROFILE ON p120

SPAIN
1 WIN 2010
PROFILE ON p121

FOCUS ON ARGENTINA

Messi, Maradona and tough-tackling hardmen!

FACT FILE

Nickname La Albiceleste (The White and Sky Blues) **Governing body** Argentine Football Association (AFA) **Confederation** CONMEBOL (South America) **Head coach** Lionel Scaloni **Captain** Lionel Messi **Home stadium** Various **First match** Uruguay 0-6 Argentina, 1902 **Biggest win** Argentina 12-0 Ecuador, 1942 **Biggest defeat** Czechoslovakia 6-1 Argentina, 1958; Bolivia 6-1 Argentina, 2009; Spain 6-1 Argentina, 2018

MOST CAPPED PLAYERS

NAME	CAPS	YEARS
1 Javier Mascherano	147	2003-18
2 Javier Zanetti	143	1994-2011
3 Lionel Messi	142	2005-present
4 Roberto Ayala	114	1994-2007
5 Diego Simeone	106	1988-2002

TOP GOALSCORERS

NAME	GOALS	YEARS
1 Lionel Messi	71	2005-present
2 Gabriel Batistuta	54	1991-2002
3 Sergio Aguero	41	2006-present
4 Hernan Crespo	35	1995-2007
5 Diego Maradona	34	1977-94

ARGENTINA ICONS

DIEGO MARADONA
Diego Armando Maradona – a man with godlike status in his homeland who became a global icon after leading Argentina to World Cup glory in 1986!

MARIO KEMPES

GABRIEL BATISTUTA

JAVIER ZANETTI

DANIEL PASSARELLA

CURRENT STAR MAN

LIONEL MESSI
For many, the best player ever. Leo has lit up tournaments, smashed every record and won every award – and done it all in his own unique style!

WORLD CUP RECORD

APPEARANCES 17
BEST RESULT Winners, 1978, 1986

FOCUS ON **BRAZIL**
Samba swagger, skilful No.10s and a superstar called Pele!

FACT FILE

Nickname Selecao (The National Team) **Governing body** Confederacao Brasileira de Futebol (CBF) **Confederation** CONMEBOL (South America) **Head coach** Tite **Captain** Thiago Silva **Home stadium** Various **First match** Argentina 3-0 Brazil, 1914 **Biggest win** Brazil 10-1 Bolivia, 1949; Brazil 9-0 Colombia, 1957 **Biggest defeat** Uruguay 6-0 Brazil, 1920; Brazil 1-7 Germany, 2014

MOST CAPPED PLAYERS

NAME	CAPS	YEARS
1 Cafu	142	1990-2006
2 Roberto Carlos	125	1992-2006
3 Dani Alves	118	2006-19
4 Lucio	105	2000-11
5 Neymar	103	2010-present

TOP GOALSCORERS

NAME	GOALS	YEARS
1 Pele	77	1957-71
2 Neymar	64	2010-present
3 Ronaldo	62	1994-2011
4 Romario	55	1987-2005
5 Zico	48	1976-86

BRAZIL ICONS

PELE
Edson Arantes do Nascimento is considered by many to be the greatest of all time. He was a prolific forward who scored more than 1,000 goals!

SOCRATES

GARRINCHA

ZICO

RONALDO

CURRENT STAR MAN

NEYMAR
The 29-year-old forward, with almost 400 career goals, became the most expensive footballer of all time when he joined PSG for £198m in 2017!

WORLD CUP RECORD
APPEARANCES 21 **BEST RESULT** Winners, 1958, 1962, 1970, 1994, 2002

FOCUS ON ENGLAND

FACT FILE

Nickname The Three Lions **Governing body** The Football Association (The FA) **Confederation** UEFA (Europe) **Head coach** Gareth Southgate **Captain** Harry Kane **Home stadium** Wembley Stadium (90,000) **First match** Scotland 0-0 England, 1872 **Biggest win** England 13-0 Ireland, 1882 **Biggest defeat** Hungary 7-1 England, 1954

MOST CAPPED PLAYERS

NAME	CAPS	YEARS
1 Peter Shilton	125	1970-90
2 Wayne Rooney	120	2003-18
3 David Beckham	115	1996-2009
4 Steven Gerrard	114	2000-14
5 Bobby Moore	108	1962-73

TOP GOALSCORERS

NAME	GOALS	YEARS
1 Wayne Rooney	53	2003-18
2 Bobby Charlton	49	1958-70
3 Gary Lineker	48	1984-92
4 Jimmy Greaves	44	1959-67
5 Michael Owen	40	1998-2008

ENGLAND ICONS

BOBBY CHARLTON This legendary attacking midfielder clocked up more than 750 games for Man. United, 106 games for England and won the Ballon d'Or in 1966!

BOBBY MOORE

WAYNE ROONEY

DAVID BECKHAM

STANLEY MATTHEWS

CURRENT STAR MAN

HARRY KANE The 2018 World Cup Golden Boot winner is arguably the world's best striker. He's on course to become the Prem's and England's all-time top scorer!

WORLD CUP RECORD

APPEARANCES 15 **BEST RESULT** Winners, 1966

The birthplace of the beautiful game – home to physical, all-action, high-tempo football!

ENGLAND'S MOST-CAPPED 11

PETER SHILTON
125 caps
1970-90

GARY NEVILLE
85 caps
1995-2007

BILLY WRIGHT
105 caps
1946-59

BOBBY MOORE
108 caps
1962-73

ASHLEY COLE
107 caps
2001-14

DAVID BECKHAM
115 caps
1996-2009

FRANK LAMPARD
106 caps
1999-2014

STEVEN GERRARD
114 caps
2000-14

BOBBY CHARLTON
106 caps
1958-70

WAYNE ROONEY
120 caps
2003-18

MICHAEL OWEN
89 caps
1998-2008

FOCUS ON FRANCE

Flamboyant frontmen and free-flowing football – c'est fantastique!

FACT FILE

Nickname Le Bleus (The Blues) **Governing body** Federation Francaise De Football (FFF) **Confederation** UEFA (Europe) **Head coach** Didier Deschamps **Captain** Hugo Lloris **Home stadium** Stade De France (80,698) **First match** Belgium 3-3 France, 1904 **Biggest win** France 10-0 Azerbaijan, 1995 **Biggest defeat** Denmark 17-1 France, 1908

MOST CAPPED PLAYERS

NAME	CAPS	YEARS
1 Lilian Thuram	142	1994-2008
2= Thierry Henry	123	1997-2010
2= Hugo Lloris	123	2008-present
4 Marcel Desailly	116	1993-2004
5 Zinedine Zidane	108	1994-2006

TOP GOALSCORERS

NAME	GOALS	YEARS
1 Thierry Henry	51	1997-2010
2 Olivier Giroud	44	2011-present
3 Michel Platini	41	1976-87
4 Antoine Griezmann	35	2014-present
5 David Trezeguet	34	1998-2008

FRANCE ICONS

ZINEDINE ZIDANE
A three-time world player of the year, Zizou was one of the most elegant playmakers ever. His touch, control, vision and tek saw him hoover up trophies!

MICHEL PLATINI

THIERRY HENRY

JEAN-PIERRE PAPIN

JUST FONTAINE

CURRENT STAR MAN

KYLIAN MBAPPE
Here's a Frenchman who could surpass the great Zidane. The rapid forward, who's got 100 goals over the past three seasons, is 100% a future legend!

WORLD CUP RECORD

APPEARANCES 15
BEST RESULT Winners 1998, 2018

FOCUS ON GERMANY
The great all-rounders – technically, physically and mentally strong!

FACT FILE

Nickname Die Mannschaft (The Team) **Governing body** Deutscher Fussball-Bund (DFB) **Confederation** UEFA (Europe) **Head coach** Hansi Flick **Captain** Manuel Neuer **Home stadium** Various **First match** Switzerland 5-3 Germany, 1908 **Biggest win** Germany 16-0 Russia, 1912 **Biggest defeat** England Amateurs 9-0 Germany, 1909

MOST CAPPED PLAYERS

NAME	CAPS	YEARS
1 Lothar Matthaus	150	1980-2000
2 Miroslav Klose	137	2001-14
3 Lukas Podolski	130	2004-17
4 B. Schweinsteiger	121	2004-16
5 Philipp Lahm	113	2004-14

TOP GOALSCORERS

NAME	GOALS	YEARS
1 Miroslav Klose	71	2001-14
2 Gerd Muller	68	1966-74
3 Lukas Podolski	49	2004-17
4= Rudi Voller	47	1982-94
4= Jurgen Klinsmann	47	1987-98

GERMANY ICONS

FRANZ BECKENBAUER The Bayern Munich great was the OG captain, leader, legend. He won 103 caps and led them to World Cup and Euros victories!

GERD MULLER — LOTHAR MATTHAUS

MIROSLAV KLOSE — PHILIPP LAHM

CURRENT STAR MAN

TONI KROOS The playmaker has been bossing it from midfield for a decade – he's won the league in Germany and Spain, and the Champions League four times!

WORLD CUP RECORD
APPEARANCES 19 **BEST RESULT** Winners, 1954, 1974, 1990, 2014

FOCUS ON ITALY

A love of tactics, technical ability and clean sheets!

FACT FILE

Nickname Azzurri (The Blues) **Governing body** Federazione Italiana Giuoco Calcio (FIGC) **Confederation** UEFA (Europe) **Head coach** Roberto Mancini **Captain** Giorgio Chiellini **Home stadium** Various **First match** Italy 6-2 France, 1910 **Biggest win** Italy 9-0 USA, 1948 **Biggest defeat** Hungary 7-1 Italy, 1924

MOST CAPPED PLAYERS

NAME	CAPS	YEARS
1 Gianluigi Buffon	176	1997-2018
2 Fabio Cannavaro	136	1997-2010
3 Paolo Maldini	126	1988-2002
4 Daniele De Rossi	117	2004-17
5 Andrea Pirlo	116	2002-15

TOP GOALSCORERS

NAME	GOALS	YEARS
1 Luigi Riva	35	1965-74
2 Giuseppe Meazza	33	1930-39
3 Silvio Piola	30	1935-52
4= Roberto Baggio	27	1988-2004
4= A. Del Piero	27	1995-2008

ITALY ICONS

PAOLO MALDINI The cool, composed centre-back/left-back played more than 900 games for AC Milan over 25 seasons, winning the Champions League five times!

ANDREA PIRLO

FRANCO BARESI

GIANLUIGI BUFFON

ROBERTO BAGGIO

CURRENT STAR MAN

CIRO IMMOBILE The Lazio forward has been one of the deadliest strikers in Serie A over the past five seasons, winning the Golden Boot twice since 2018!

WORLD CUP RECORD

APPEARANCES 18 **BEST RESULT** Winners 1934, 1938, 1982, 2006

FOCUS ON SPAIN

Midfield magicians, incredible tek – the kings of possession footy!

FACT FILE

Nickname La Furia Roja (The Red Fury) **Governing body** Real Federacion Espanola De Futbol (RFEF) **Confederation** UEFA (Europe) **Head coach** Luis Enrique **Captain** Sergio Ramos **Home stadium** various **First match** Spain 1-0 Denmark, 1920 **Biggest win** Spain 13-0 Bulgaria, 1933 **Biggest defeat** Spain 1-7 Italy, 1928; England 7-1 Spain, 1931

MOST CAPPED PLAYERS

NAME	CAPS	YEARS
1 Sergio Ramos	180	2005-present
2 Iker Casillas	167	2000-16
3 Xavi	133	2000-14
4 Andres Iniesta	131	2006-18
5 Andoni Zubizarreta	126	1985-98

TOP GOALSCORERS

NAME	GOALS	YEARS
1 David Villa	59	2005-17
2 Raul	44	1996-2006
3 Fernando Torres	38	2003-14
4 David Silva	35	2006-18
5 Fernando Hierro	29	1989-2002

SPAIN ICONS!

XAVI
Barcelona and Spain's best-ever midfielder – and the heartbeat of both teams. Xavi was the man who led the tiki-taka takeover of world football!

RAUL

ANDRES INIESTA

DAVID VILLA

ALFREDO DI STEFANO

CURRENT STAR MAN

THIAGO ALCANTARA
Another midfield baller off the Spanish production line. The Liverpool playmaker has also starred for Barcelona and Bayern Munich!

WORLD CUP RECORD

APPEARANCES 15
BEST RESULT Winners, 2010

FOCUS ON URUGUAY

The first World Cup winners – fearsome in attack and in defence!

FACT FILE

Nickname La Celeste (The Sky Blue) **Governing body** Asociacion Uruguaya De Futbol (AUF) **Confederation** CONMEBOL (South America) **Head coach** Oscar Tabarez **Captain** Diego Godin **Home stadium** Estadio Centenario (60,235) **First match** Uruguay 0-6 Argentina, 1902 **Biggest win** Uruguay 9-0 Bolivia, 1927 **Biggest defeat** Uruguay 0-6 Argentina, 1902

MOST CAPPED PLAYERS

NAME	CAPS	YEARS
1 Diego Godin	139	2005-present
2 Maxi Pereira	125	2005-18
3 Edinson Cavani	118	2008-present
4= Fernando Muslera	116	2009-present
4= Luis Suarez	116	2007-present

TOP GOALSCORERS

NAME	GOALS	YEARS
1 Luis Suarez	63	2007-present
2 Edinson Cavani	51	2008-present
3 Diego Forlan	36	2002-14
4 Hector Scarone	31	1917-30
5 Angel Romano	28	1913-27

URUGUAY ICONS

ENZO FRANCESCOLI El Principe (The Prince) was a classy playmaker, who was a genius on the ball and was South American Footballer of the Year twice!

DIEGO GODIN

JUAN A. SCHIAFFINO

EDINSON CAVANI

DIEGO FORLAN

CURRENT STAR MAN

LUIS SUAREZ One of the most lethal strikers in recent times, the Atletico Madrid man was born to score. He's bagged more than 500 goals for club and country!

WORLD CUP RECORD

APPEARANCES 13
BEST RESULT Winners 1930, 1950

NOW, FOR THE HOME NATIONS & REPUBLIC OF IRELAND!

TURN OVER NOW!

NORTHERN IRELAND
PAGE 124

SCOTLAND
PAGE 126

REPUBLIC OF IRELAND
PAGE 125

WALES
PAGE 127

FOCUS ON NORTHERN IRELAND
The land of George Best and the Green And White Army!

FACT FILE

Nickname Norn Iron **Governing body** Irish Football Association (IFA) **Confederation** UEFA (Europe) **Head coach** Ian Baraclough **Captain** Steven Davis **Home stadium** Windsor Park (18,614) **First match** N. Ireland 1-4 England, 1950 **Biggest win** N. Ireland 5-0 Cyprus, 1971; Faroe Islands 0-5 N. Ireland, 1991 **Biggest defeat** Holland 6-0 N. Ireland, 2012

MOST CAPPED PLAYERS

NAME	CAPS	YEARS
1 Steven Davis	126	2005-present
2 Pat Jennings	119	1964-86
3 Aaron Hughes	112	1998-2018
4 David Healy	95	2000-13
5 Jonny Evans	91	2006-present

TOP GOALSCORERS!

NAME	GOALS	YEARS
1 David Healy	36	2000-13
2 Kyle Lafferty	20	2006-present
3= Billy Gillespie	13	1913-32
3= Colin Clarke	13	1986-93
5 Five players	12	

NORTHERN IRELAND ICONS

GEORGE BEST
Britain's best-ever player, this Ballon d'Or-winning Man. United legend was a genius, tying defenders in knots with his fast and skilful dribbling!

DANNY BLANCHFLOWER

PAT JENNINGS

MARTIN O'NEILL

DAVID HEALY

CURRENT STAR MAN

JONNY EVANS
A calm, composed centre-back whose consistency and reading of the game has seen him clock up more than 400 Prem games for four different clubs!

WORLD CUP RECORD

APPEARANCES 3
BEST RESULT Quarter-finals, 1958

FOCUS ON REP. OF IRELAND

The team of Big Jack, the Keanes and fighting spirit!

FACT FILE

Nickname The Boys In Green **Governing body** Football Association Of Ireland (FAI) **Confederation** UEFA (Europe) **Head coach** Stephen Kenny **Captain** Seamus Coleman **Home stadium** Aviva Stadium (51,700) **First match** Ireland 1-0 Bulgaria, 1924 **Biggest win** Republic Of Ireland 8-0 Malta, 1983 **Biggest defeat** Brazil 7-0 Republic Of Ireland, 1982

MOST CAPPED PLAYERS

NAME	CAPS	YEARS
1 Robbie Keane	146	1998-2016
2 Shay Given	134	1996-2016
3 John O'Shea	118	2001-18
4 Kevin Kilbane	110	1997-2011
5 Steve Staunton	102	1998-2002

TOP GOALSCORERS

NAME	GOALS	YEARS
1 Robbie Keane	68	1998-2016
2 Niall Quinn	21	1986-2002
3 Frank Stapleton	20	1977-90
4= Don Givens	19	1969-81
4= John Aldridge	19	1986-97
4= Tony Cascarino	19	1985-2000

REPUBLIC OF IRELAND ICONS

ROBBIE KEANE
The striker played for 11 clubs in his 21-year career, including Tottenham and Inter Milan. He's got more international goals than Neymar and Zlatan Ibrahimovic!

ROY KEANE

LIAM BRADY

PAUL McGRATH

RAY HOUGHTON

CURRENT STAR MAN

SEAMUS COLEMAN
The 32-year-old, who's played more than 300 games for Everton since 2009, has been one of the Prem's best right-backs for the past decade!

WORLD CUP RECORD

APPEARANCES 3
BEST RESULT Quarter-finals, 1990

FOCUS ON SCOTLAND

Passion, commitment and desire, roared on by the Tartan Army!

FACT FILE

Nickname Tartan Army **Governing body** Scottish Football Association (SFA) **Confederation** UEFA (Europe) **Head coach** Steve Clarke **Captain** Andrew Robertson **Home stadium** Hampden Park (51,866) **First match** Scotland 0-0 England, 1872 **Biggest win** Scotland 11-0 Ireland, 1901 **Biggest defeat** Uruguay 7-0 Scotland, 1954

MOST CAPPED PLAYERS

NAME	CAPS	YEARS
1 Kenny Dalglish	102	1971-86
2 Jim Leighton	91	1982-98
3 Darren Fletcher	80	2003-17
4 Alex McLeish	77	1980-93
5 Paul McStay	76	1983-97

TOP GOALSCORERS

NAME	GOALS	YEARS
1= Denis Law	30	1958-74
1= Kenny Dalglish	30	1971-86
3 Hughie Gallacher	24	1924-35
4 Lawrie Reilly	22	1948-57
5 Ally McCoist	19	1986-98

SCOTLAND ICONS

KENNY DALGLISH The ex-Celtic and Liverpool forward, who won ten league titles in his career, is a legend for Scotland – no-one has played more games or scored more goals!

DENIS LAW

GRAEME SOUNESS

JIMMY JOHNSTONE

BILLY BREMNER

CURRENT STAR MAN

ANDREW ROBERTSON The rampaging Liverpool star is one of best left-backs in Europe –he's got 37 assists in the past four seasons. Phenomenal!

WORLD CUP RECORD

APPEARANCES 8
BEST RESULT Group stage, eight times

FOCUS ON **WALES**

Drive, determination and a sprinkling of genuine top-class talent!

FACT FILE

Nickname The Dragons **Governing body** Football Association Of Wales (FAW) **Confederation** UEFA (Europe) **Head coach** Rob Page (caretaker) **Captain** Gareth Bale **Home stadium** Cardiff City Stadium (33,280) **First match** Scotland 4-0 Wales, 1876 **Biggest win** Wales 11-0 Ireland, 1888 **Biggest defeat** Scotland 9-0 Wales, 1878

MOST CAPPED PLAYERS

NAME	CAPS	YEARS
1 Chris Gunter	100	2007-present
2 Wayne Hennessey	95	2007-present
3 Neville Southall	92	1982-97
4 Gareth Bale	90	2006-present
5 Ashley Williams	86	2008-19

TOP GOALSCORERS

NAME	GOALS	YEARS
1 Gareth Bale	33	2006-present
2 Ian Rush	28	1980-96
3= Trevor Ford	23	1947-57
3= Ivor Allchurch	23	1951-66
5 Dean Saunders	22	1986-2001

WALES ICONS

JOHN CHARLES The Wales striker was a hero at Leeds, where he once hit a record 42 goals in 39 games in a season, and at Juventus, where he won Serie A three times!

JOHN TOSHACK

IAN RUSH

MARK HUGHES

RYAN GIGGS

CURRENT STAR MAN

GARETH BALE The skipper is one of footy's biggest stars, scoring some unbelievable goals, winning trophies and becoming Real Madrid's record signing in 2013!

WORLD CUP RECORD

APPEARANCES 1
BEST RESULT Quarter-finals, 1958

THE LANGUAGE

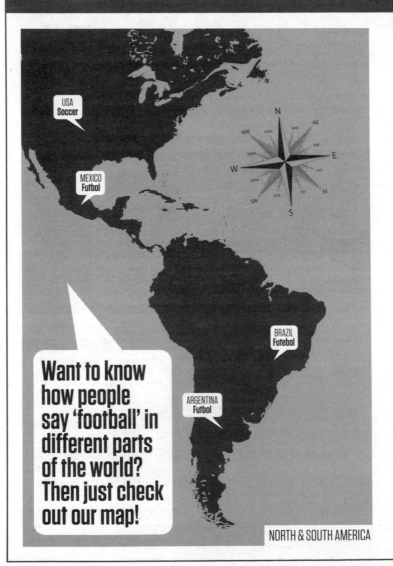

OF FOOTBALL

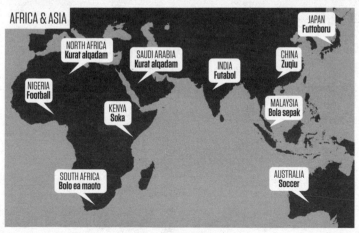

EUROPEAN

Whether you refer to it as the UEFA European Championship or simply the Euros, this is the main competition for European nations – with the winners being crowned the champions of Europe!

■ The first European Championship was held in France in 1960 and there has been a tournament every four years since – apart from 2020, when it was postponed due to the Covid pandemic.

There have been 15 tournaments to date, which have produced ten different champions – only France and Italy have hosted it more than once.

The first five tournaments featured just four teams, but it's grown since then – now 24 teams battle it out over a month to see who really is the best team in Europe!

CHAMPIONSHIP

The Euros has given us some of the most memorable moments in football history!

Wanna know why this guy is a total Euros legend? You're about to find out!

CR7 has written his name into the Euros history books – but how has he done it?

EURO CHAMPIONSHIP

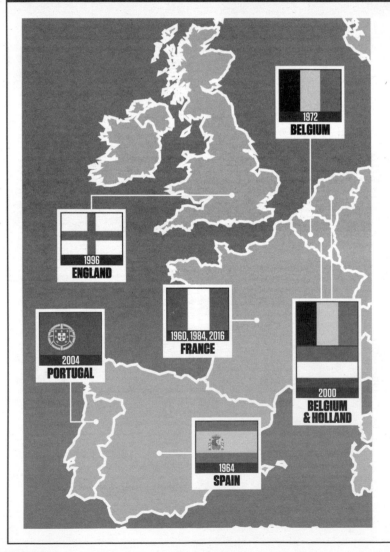

1972
BELGIUM

1996
ENGLAND

1960, 1984, 2016
FRANCE

2004
PORTUGAL

2000
BELGIUM & HOLLAND

1964
SPAIN

HOST NATIONS

1992
SWEDEN

1988
WEST GERMANY

2012
POLAND & UKRAINE

2008
AUSTRIA & SWITZERLAND

1968, 1980
ITALY

1976
YUGOSLAVIA

EURO 1960 FRANCE

The one... that kicked it all off!

FINAL POSITIONS

Winners **Soviet Union**
Runners-up **Yugoslavia**
Third place **Czechoslovakia**
Fourth place **France**

TOP SCORERS

1= Valentin Ivanov
Soviet Union **2 goals**
1= Francois Heutte
France **2 goals**
1= Viktor Ponedelnik
Soviet Union **2 goals**
1= Milan Galic Yugoslavia **2 goals**
1= Drazan Jerkovic Yugoslavia **2 goals**

THE FINAL

SOVIET UNION 2-1 (AET) YUGOSLAVIA

Metreveli 49,
Ponedelnik 113

Galic 43

Date 10 July 1960 **Venue** Parc Des Princes, Paris
Referee Arthur Edward Ellis (England) **Attendance** 17,966

CHAMPIONS SOVIET UNION

GOLDEN BOOT
5 players
on 2 goals

PLAYER OF THE TOURNAMENT
N/A

EURO 1964 SPAIN

The one... where Spain won their first ever trophy!

FINAL POSITIONS

Winners **Spain**
Runners-up **Soviet Union**
Third place **Hungary**
Fourth place **Denmark**

TOP SCORERS

1= Ferenc Bene
Hungary **2 goals**
1= Dezso Novak
Hungary **2 goals**
1= Jesus Maria Pereda
Spain **2 goals**

THE FINAL

SPAIN 2-1 SOVIET UNION

Pereda 6,
Marcelino 84

Khusainov 8

Date 21 June 1964 **Venue** Santiago Bernabeu, Madrid
Referee Arthur Holland (England) **Attendance** 79,115

CHAMPIONS SPAIN

GOLDEN BOOT
3 players
on 2 goals

PLAYER OF THE TOURNAMENT
N/A

EURO 1968 ITALY

The one... England entered for the very first time!

FINAL POSITIONS

Winners **Italy**
Runners-up **Yugoslavia**
Third place **England**
Fourth place **Soviet Union**

TOP SCORERS

1 **Dragan Dzajic**
Yugoslavia **2 goals**
2= **Bobby Charlton**
& Geoff Hurst
England **1 goal**
2= **P. Anastasi** Italy
1 goal 2= **A. Domenghini** Italy **1 goal**

THE FINAL (REPLAY, FIRST MATCH FINISHED 1-1)

ITALY 2-0 YUGOSLAVIA

Riva 12,
Anastasi 31

Date 10 June 1968 **Venue** Stadio Olimpico, Rome
Referee Jose Maria Ortiz (Spain) **Attendance** 32,886

CHAMPIONS ITALY

GOLDEN BOOT
Dragan Dzajic
Yugoslavia

PLAYER OF THE TOURNAMENT
N/A

EURO 1972 BELGIUM

The one... that was all about Gerd Muller!

FINAL POSITIONS

Winners **West Germany**
Runners-up **Soviet Union**
Third place **Belgium**
Fourth place **Hungary**

TOP SCORERS

1 **Gerd Muller** West Germany **4 goals**
2= **Raoul Lambert** Belgium **1 goal**
2= **Odilon Polleunis** Belgium **1 goal**
2= **Paul Van Himst** Belgium **1 goal**
2= **Lajos Ku** Hungary **1 goal**
2= **Anatoliy Konkov** Soviet Union **1 goal**
2= **H. Wimmer** West Germany **1 goal**

THE FINAL

WEST GERMANY 3-0 SOVIET UNION

Muller 27, 58,
Wimmer 52

Date 18 June 1972 **Venue** Heysel Stadium, Brussels
Referee Ferdinand Marschall (Austria) **Attendance** 43,066

CHAMPIONS WEST GERMANY

GOLDEN BOOT
Gerd Muller
West Germany

PLAYER OF THE TOURNAMENT
N/A

EURO 1976 YUGOSLAVIA

The one... that saw the birth of the Panenka penalty!

THE FINAL

CZECHOSLOVAKIA **2-2** WEST GERMANY
(AET)

Svehlik 8,
Dobias 25

CZECHOSLOVAKIA WON 5-3 ON PENALTIES

Muller 28,
Holzenbein 89

Date 20 June 1976 **Venue** Red Star Stadium, Belgrade
Referee Sergio Gonella (Italy) **Attendance** 30,790

CHAMPIONS CZECHOSLOVAKIA

FINAL POSITIONS
Winners **Czechoslovakia**
Runners-up **West Germany**
Third place **Holland**
Fourth place **Yugoslavia**

TOP SCORERS

1 Dieter Muller
West Germany **4 goals**
2= **Ruud Geels**
Holland **2 goals**
2= **Dragan Dzajic**
Yugoslavia **2 goals**

GOLDEN BOOT
Dieter Muller
West Germany

PLAYER OF THE TOURNAMENT
N/A

EURO 1980 ITALY

The one... where Germany reclaimed the Euro crown!

THE FINAL

BELGIUM **1-2** WEST GERMANY

Vandereycken 75
(pen)

Hrubesch 10, 88

Date 22 June 1980 **Venue** Stadio Olimpico, Rome
Referee Nicolae Rainea (Romania) **Attendance** 47,860

CHAMPIONS WEST GERMANY

FINAL POSITIONS
Winners **West Germany**
Runners-up **Belgium**
Third place **Czechoslovakia**
Fourth place **Italy**

TOP SCORERS

1 Klaus Allofs West
Germany **3 goals**
2= Zdenek Nehoda
Czechoslovakia
2 goals 2= Kees Kist
Holland **2 goals**
2= Horst Hrubesch West Germany **2 goals**

GOLDEN BOOT
Klaus Allofs
West Germany

PLAYER OF THE TOURNAMENT
N/A

EURO 1984 FRANCE

The one... where Michel Platini became a legend!

TOP SCORERS
1 **Michel Platini** France **9 goals**
2 **Frank Arnesen** Denmark **3 goals**
3 **Five players on 2 goals**

THE FINAL

FRANCE 2-0 SPAIN

Platini 57,
Bellone 90

Date 27 June 1984 **Venue** Parc Des Princes, Paris
Referee Vojtech Christov (Czechoslovakia) **Attendance** 47,368

CHAMPIONS FRANCE

GOLDEN BOOT
Michel Platini
France

PLAYER OF THE TOURNAMENT
Michel Platini
France

EURO 1988 WEST GERMANY

The one... where Marco van Basten scored *that* goal!

TOP SCORERS
1 **Marco van Basten** Holland **5 goals**
2= **Oleh Protasov** Soviet Union **2 goals**
2= **Rudi Voller** West Germany **2 goals**

THE FINAL

SOVIET UNION 0-2 HOLLAND

Gullit 32,
Van Basten 54

Date 25 June 1988 **Venue** Olympiastadion, Munich
Referee Michel Vautrot (France) **Attendance** 62,770

CHAMPIONS HOLLAND

GOLDEN BOOT
Marco van
Basten Holland

PLAYER OF THE TOURNAMENT
Marco van Basten
Holland

THE MAN BEHIND THE EUROS

HENRI DELAUNAY

This French dude was the first general secretary of UEFA, and the European Championship was his idea – but he sadly died five years before the first tournament!

EURO 1960

NEW ERA Czech keeper Viliam Schrojf makes a save against a Soviet Union player during the very first Euros, which was won by the Soviets!

EURO 1984

PLAT'S MAGIC Michel Platini curls in the opening goal of the final – his ninth of the tournament – to set France on the way to a 2-0 win over Spain!

EURO 1988

DUTCH DELIGHT Marco van Basten spectacularly volleys home to seal a 2-0 win over the Soviet Union in the final!

MVB THE MVP Van Basten, who was only 23 at the time, finished Euro 88 as the top scorer and was named Player of the Tournament!

EURO 1992

DANISH DYNAMITE Rank outsiders Denmark celebrate an improbable fairytale win over Germany in the final of Euro 92!

EURO 1992 SWEDEN

The one... where Denmark stunned the world!

THE FINAL

DENMARK **2-0** **GERMANY**

Jensen 18,
Vilfort 78

Date 26 June 1992 **Venue** Ullevi, Gothenburg
Referee Bruno Galler (Switzerland) **Attendance** 37,800

WINNERS DENMARK

TOP SCORERS
1= **Henrik Larsen** Denmark **3 goals**
1= **Dennis Bergkamp** Holland **3 goals**
1= **Karl-Heinz Riedle** Germany **3 goals**
1= **Tomas Brolin** Sweden **3 goals**

GOLDEN BOOT
**4 players
on 3 goals**

PLAYER OF THE TOURNAMENT
Peter Schmeichel
Denmark

EURO 2000 BELGIUM & HOLLAND

The one... won by France with a golden goal!

THE FINAL

FRANCE **2-1** (AET) **ITALY**

Wiltord 90,   Delvecchio 55
Trezeguet 103

Date 2 July 2000 **Venue** De Kuip, Rotterdam
Referee Anders Frisk (Sweden) **Attendance** 48,200

WINNERS FRANCE

TOP SCORERS
1= **Savo Milosevic** Yugoslavia **5 goals**
1= **Patrick Kluivert** Holland **5 goals**
2 **Nuno Gomes** Portugal **4 goals**

GOLDEN BOOT
Savo Milosevic
Yugoslavia & **Patrick
Kluivert** Holland

PLAYER OF THE TOURNAMENT
Zinedine Zidane
France

EURO 1996 ENGLAND

The one... where football nearly came home!

TOP SCORERS

1 **Alan Shearer** England **5 goals**
2= **Hristo Stoichkov** Bulgaria **3 goals**
2= **Davor Suker** Croatia **3 goals**
2= **Brian Laudrup** Denmark **3 goals**
2= **Jurgen Klinsmann** Germany **3 goals**

THE STORY OF THE THREE LIONS

Footy fever swept England in the summer of 1996, the first time a football tournament had been held in the country since the 1966 World Cup. England stormed to the semis – but it was to end in heartbreak, as they lost on penalties in the semi-final to Germany, with Gareth Southgate missing the vital spot-kick!

ENGLAND'S RESULTS

Group A England 1-1 Switzerland
Group A Scotland 0-2 England
Group A Holland 1-4 England
Quarter-finals Spain 0-0 England
(England win 4-2 on penalties)
Semi-finals Germany 1-1 England
(Germany win 6-5 on penalties)

THE FINAL

CZECH REPUBLIC 1-2 GERMANY

Berger 59 (pen) GERMANY WON WITH A GOLDEN GOAL **Bierhoff 73, 95**

Date 30 June 1996 **Venue** Wembley Stadium, London
Referee Pierluigi Pairetto (Italy) **Attendance** 73,611

WINNERS GERMANY

GOLDEN BOOT
Alan Shearer
England

PLAYER OF THE TOURNAMENT
Matthias Sammer
Germany

ENGLAND'S EURO 96 LINE-UP

Seaman
Southgate
Adams
Anderton
Ince
Pearce
Gascoigne
Platt
Sheringham
McManaman
Shearer

EURO 2004 PORTUGAL

The one... **where unfancied Greece pulled off a shock!**

TOP SCORERS
1 Milan Baros Czech Republic **5 goals**
2= Wayne Rooney England **4 goals**
2= Ruud van Nistelrooy Holland **4 goals**

THE FINAL

PORTUGAL 0-1 GREECE

Charisteas 57

Date 4 July 2004 **Venue** Estadio Da Luz, Lisbon
Referee Marcus Merk (Germany) **Attendance** 62,865

CHAMPIONS GREECE

GOLDEN BOOT
Milan Baros
Czech Republic

PLAYER OF THE TOURNAMENT
Theodoros Zagorakis
Greece

EURO 2008 AUSTRIA & SWITZERLAND

The one... **where tiki-taka Spain took the throne!**

TOP SCORERS
1 David Villa Spain **4 goals**
2= Lukas Podolski Germany **3 goals**
2= Roman Pavlyuchenko Russia **3 goals**
2= Hakan Yakin Switzerland **3 goals**
2= Semih Senturk Turkey **3 goals**

THE FINAL

GERMANY 0-1 SPAIN

Torres 33

Date 29 June 2008 **Venue** Ernst-Happel-Stadion, Vienna
Referee Roberto Rosetti (Italy) **Attendance** 51,428

CHAMPIONS SPAIN

GOLDEN BOOT
David Villa
Spain

PLAYER OF THE TOURNAMENT
Xavi
Spain

EURO 2012 POLAND & UKRAINE

The one... when classy Spain turned it on again!

TOP SCORERS

1= **Mario Mandzukic** Croatia **3 goals**
1= **Mario Gomez** Germany **3 goals**
1= **Mario Balotelli** Italy **3 goals**
1= **Cristiano Ronaldo** Portugal **3 goals**
1= **Alan Dzagoev** Russia **3 goals**
1= **Fernando Torres** Spain **3 goals**

THE FINAL

SPAIN	4-0	ITALY

Silva 14, Alba 41, Torres 84, Mata 88

Date 1 July 2012 **Venue** Olympic Stadium, Kiev
Referee Pedro Proença (Portugal) **Attendance** 63,170

CHAMPIONS SPAIN

GOLDEN BOOT	*PLAYER OF THE TOURNAMENT*
Fernando Torres* Spain	Andres Iniesta Spain

*BASED ON MINUTES PER GOAL

EURO 2016 FRANCE

The one... with final heartbreak for the hosts!

TOP SCORERS

1 **Antoine Griezmann** France **6 goals**
2= **Olivier Giroud** France **3 goals**
2= **Dimitri Payet** France **3 goals**
2= **Cristiano Ronaldo** Portugal **3 goals**
2= **Nani** Portugal **3 goals**
2= **Alvaro Morata** Spain **3 goals**
2= **Gareth Bale** Wales **3 goals**

THE FINAL

PORTUGAL	1-0 (AET)	FRANCE

Eder 109

Date 10 July 2016 **Venue** Stade De France, Saint-Denis
Referee Mark Clattenburg (England) **Attendance** 75,868

CHAMPIONS PORTUGAL

GOLDEN BOOT	*PLAYER OF THE TOURNAMENT*
Antoine Griezmann France	Antoine Griezmann France

EURO 1996

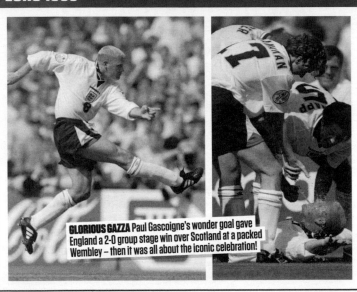

GLORIOUS GAZZA Paul Gascoigne's wonder goal gave England a 2-0 group stage win over Scotland at a packed Wembley – then it was all about the iconic celebration!

EURO 2004

ROO'S THE MAN 18-year-old Wayne Rooney burst onto the world scene at Euro 2004 – scoring four goals, including this one against Croatia!

GREEK GODS Angelos Charisteas wheels away in delight after scoring the only goal of the 2004 final against hosts Portugal – Greece's victory was one of the biggest upsets of all time!

EURO 2008

SPAIN REIGN Fernando Torres' first-half goal was enough to secure a 1-0 win for Spain over Germany in the 2008 final – their first trophy for 44 years!

EURO 2012

THE KING OF COOL England's quarter-final against Italy finished 0-0 and went to penalties – that's when Andrea Pirlo pulled out the cheekiest of all Panenkas as Italy won 4-2!

SUPER MARIO Italy striker Mario Balotelli scored twice in a 2-1 semi-final win over Germany and celebrated in style!

EURO CHAMPIONSHIP

HOLLAND
1 WIN 1988

PORTUGAL
1 WIN 2016

FRANCE
2 WINS 1984, 2000

SPAIN
3 WINS 1964, 2008, 2012

WINNERS

DENMARK
1 WIN 1992

SOVIET UNION
1 WIN 1960

GERMANY
3 WINS 1972, 1980, 1996

CZECHOSLOVAKIA
1 WIN 1976

GREECE
1 WIN 2004

ITALY
1 WIN 1968

EUROPEAN CHAMPIONSHIP

These guys have scored more goals at the European Championships than anyone else in the history of the tournament!

PLAYER	COUNTRY	GOALS	GAMES	TOURNAMENTS
1= Michel Platini	France	9	5	1984
1= Cristiano Ronaldo	Portugal	9	21	2004, 2008, 2012, 2016
3 Alan Shearer	England	7	9	1992, 1996, 2000
4= Antoine Griezmann	France	6	7	2016
4= Ruud van Nistelrooy	Holland	6	8	2004, 2008
4= Patrick Kluivert	Holland	6	9	1996, 2000
4= Wayne Rooney	England	6	10	2004, 2012, 2016
4= Thierry Henry	France	6	11	2000, 2004, 2008
4= Zlatan Ibrahimovic	Sweden	6	13	2004, 2008, 2012, 2016
4= Nuno Gomes	Portugal	6	14	2000, 2004, 2008

WHO IS CRISTIANO RONALDO?

This guy needs no introduction – he's a living legend of the game. The Juventus star, who made his debut at the Euros back in 2004, is Portugal's all-time top scorer and their appearance holder – and he fired his country to glory at Euro 2016. Here are five huge facts that you may not know about CR7!

■ He is the only European player to score more than 100 goals for his country!

■ He has won the league and been Player of the Year in England, Spain and Italy!

■ In 2018, he became the first player to win the Champions League five times!

■ He was 23 when he won the Ballon d'Or for the first time – he's now won it five times in total!

■ He's scored more goals in Euro qualifiers than any other player – he's bagged 31 in total!

TOP SCORERS

WHO IS MICHEL PLATINI?

The man tied with Cristiano Ronaldo at the top of the Euros scoring charts is a French icon – a playmaking, goalscoring, match-winning genius. Platini was a true superstar in the 1970s and 1980s, but only played at the Euros once. Here are five facts you seriously need to know about him!

■ He played for Nancy, Saint-Etienne and Juventus – and was nicknamed Le Roi, which means the King!

■ He was top scorer in Serie A three years in a row from 1983 to 1985!

■ He won the Ballon d'Or three times in a row – also in 1983, 1984 and 1985!

■ He scored in every game at Euro 1984 as France were crowned champions, he won the Golden Boot and was Player of the Tournament!

■ He bagged an 18-minute hat-trick at Euro '84 in France's 3-2 group-stage win over Yugoslavia!

ALAN SHEARER

The Golden Boot winner at Euro '96, who also got two at Euro 2000, is England's top scorer at the Euros!

EUROPEAN CHAMPIONSHIP

C-RON – THE EUROS GOAT!

As well as his nine tournament goals, CR7 has also bagged 31 qualifying goals. This gives him a record-breaking total of 40 goals in Euros finals and qualifiers.

MOST EUROPEAN CHAMPIONSHIP GOALS (INCLUDING QUALIFYING)

1 Cristiano Ronaldo Portugal **40 goals**
2 Zlatan Ibrahimovic Sweden **25 goals**
3 Robbie Keane Rep. Of Ireland **23 goals**

MOST EUROPEAN CHAMPIONSHIP APPEARANCES

Not only has no-one scored more Euros goals than CR7, no-one has played as many tournament games as him either!
1 Cristiano Ronaldo Portugal **21 games**
2 B. Schweinsteiger Germany **18 games**
3 Gianluigi Buffon Italy **17 games**

THE YOUNG GUNS

The youngest player to ever play at the Euros is ex-Newcastle loan star Jetro Willems. The Holland left-back was just 18 years and 71 days old when he played against Denmark at Euro 2012!

Interestingly, the youngest player to appear in a Euros final is another former Premier League loanee. Renato Sanches, who spent an unhappy season at Swansea in 2017-18, was 18 years and 328 days when he helped Portugal beat France 1-0 in the final of Euro 2016!

THE GOLDEN OLDIES

Ex-Crystal Palace, Aston Villa and Burnley keeper Gabor Kiraly is the oldest player to play at the Euros. Kiraly, famous for wearing baggy tracky bottoms, was 40 years and 86 days when his Hungary team lost 4-0 to Belgium at Euro 2016!

Continuing on the ex-Premier League keeper theme, the oldest player to appear in a Euros final is Arsenal legend Jens Lehmann. The German shot-stopper, who clocked up 199 games for the Gunners, was 38 years and 232 days old when he played for Germany in their 2008 defeat by Spain!

THE BIGGEST WIN

Holland's 6-1 thumping of Yugoslavia in the quarter-finals of Euro 2000 is the biggest-ever win at the Euros!

TOP TRIVIA

THE GERMAN POWERHOUSE!

The undisputed Euro kings are Germany. They've reached the final a record six times, lifted the trophy on three occasions and hold a whole host of other records, too...

MOST EURO TOURNAMENTS

1 Germany, **13 tournaments**
2 Russia, 12 tournaments
3 Spain, 11 tournaments

MOST MATCHES PLAYED

1 Germany, **49 matches**
2 Spain, 40 matches
3 France, 39 matches

MOST WINS

1 Germany, **26 wins**
2 France, 20 wins
3 Spain, 19 wins

MOST GOALS SCORED

1 Germany, **72 goals**
2 France, 62 goals
3 Holland, 57 goals

MOST GOALS SCORED IN ONE TOURNAMENT

COUNTRY France, 1984 **14 goals**
PLAYER Michel Platini, 1984 **9 goals**

Did you know? France is the only country to host the Euros three times – in 1960, 1984 and 2016!

THE BATTLE OF THE BROTHERS

Granit Xhaka of Switzerland and Albania's Taulant Xhaka became the first brothers to play AGAINST each other in European Championship history, when the two countries met in Euro 2016!

A LEGEND IS BORN

The Panenka penalty – the cheeky dink down the middle – was born when the Euro '76 final between Czechoslovakia and West Germany went to pens. With a chance to win it, Czech midfielder Antonin Panenka ran up and casually chipped in the winning spot-kick!

CONTINENTAL CHAMPIONSHIPS

The Euros is just one of nine continental tournaments for national teams that take place every two to four years around the world. These competitions see countries from the same federations go head-to-head with the dream of being crowned that continent's champion. The biggest and most famous of these tournaments are the following...

COPA AMERICA
SEE PAGE 153
AFRICA CUP OF NATIONS
SEE PAGE 154
AFC ASIAN CUP
SEE PAGE 155
CONCACAF GOLD CUP
SEE PAGE 155

THE OTHER TOURNAMENTS!

AFRICA CAF AFRICAN NATIONS CHAMPIONSHIP
Founded 2009 **Teams** 16
Competition to find the best team in Africa – but only featuring players who play their club football in their domestic league.

NORTH AMERICA CONCACAF NATIONS LEAGUE
Founded 2018 **Teams** 41
Teams from North and Central America compete in a mixture of mini-league and knockout games to determine who will be the champion.

OCEANIA OFC NATIONS CUP
Founded 1973 **Teams** 8
Played every four years to find the champions of Oceania – won a record five times by New Zealand.

EUROPE UEFA NATIONS LEAGUE
Founded 2018 **Teams** 55
Introduced to replace meaningless friendlies, this competition is held every two years. Portugal were the first winners in 2019.

THE COPA AMERICA

- CONMEBOL -
COPA AMERICA
ARGENTINA **2021** COLOMBIA

This is the main football tournament contested by South American countries. The first one was held 105 years ago, in 1916, making it the oldest international football competition. The winners are crowned the champions of South America – but since the 1990s, countries from North America and Asia, including Australia, Japan and Qatar, have also been invited to take part!

WHO'S WON IT THE MOST TIMES?

Surprisingly, it's not the traditional superpowers of Brazil and Argentina who have been South American champions the most – it's Uruguay, although they have only won one of the past ten tournaments!

1 Uruguay	**15**
2 Argentina	14
3 Brazil	**9**
4= Paraguay	2
4= Chile	**2**
4= Peru	2
7= Colombia	**1**
7= Bolivia	1

Luis Suarez led Uruguay to their 15th win in 2011!

AFRICA CUP OF NATIONS

This is the main football tournament for African countries. It was first held 64 years ago, way back in 1957, when only three nations competed for the title – Egypt, Sudan and Ethiopia. The competition has grown a lot over the years – since 2017, 24 countries have battled it out in the finals to decide who will be crowned the champions of Africa!

WHO'S WON IT THE MOST TIMES?

Fourteen nations have been crowned champions of Africa – and it's Mohamed Salah's Egypt who have won it the most times. It's actually been 11 years since the north African country got their hands on the trophy – and that was a whole year before Mo made his international debut for the Pharaohs!

1 Egypt	7	
2 Cameroon	5	
3 Ghana	4	
4 Nigeria	3	
5= Ivory Coast	2	
5= Algeria	2	
5= DR Congo	2	
8= Zambia	1	
8= Tunisia	1	
8= Sudan	1	
8= Ethiopia	1	
8= Morocco	1	
8= South Africa	1	
8= Congo	1	

Egypt became seven-time AFCON champs in 2010!

AFC ASIAN CUP

This international tournament is for countries that are part of the Asian Football Confederation, which now includes Australia. It was first held in 1956, making it the second-oldest international competition, behind the Copa America. It's held every four years and currently features 24 different countries!

AFC ASIAN CUP™

Nine countries have been crowned champions of Asia – and it's Japan who have won it the most times. They have won four of the last eight tournaments, but Qatar are the reigning champions after their victory in 2019!

WHO'S WON IT THE MOST TIMES?

1 Japan		4
2= Saudi Arabia		3
2= Iran		3
4 South Korea		2
5= Israel		1
5= Kuwait		1
5= Australia		1
5= Iraq		1
5= Qatar		1

CONCACAF GOLD CUP

This is the main football competition for national teams based in North America, Central America and the Caribbean. The Gold Cup, which was first held 58 years ago in 1963 and took place in El Salvador, is held every two years. Since the last tournament in 2019, 16 countries have been competing for the trophy!

Concacaf **GOLD CUP**

The Gold Cup has been bossed by Mexico and the USA, who've won 14 of the last 15 tournaments between them. Mexico beat the USA 1-0 in the 2019 final, with a goal from ex-Barcelona midfielder Jonathan Dos Santos!

WHO'S WON IT THE MOST TIMES?

1 Mexico		11
2 USA		6
3 Costa Rica		3
4 Canada		2
5= Guatemala		1
5= Haiti		1
5= Honduras		1

THE A-Z OF KEY FOOTBALL

NUMBERS

10 The iconic shirt number worn by a player who is a team's chief playmaker and creative threat. The No.10 plays in the hole between midfield and attack

12th man The fans of a club. Football teams have 11 players – but a vocal, enthusiastic and passionate support can have the effect of an extra player

50/50 When two players crunch into a challenge for a loose ball at the same time – and both players have a 50% chance of winning the ball

A

Against the run of play When a team, which is clearly being outplayed, scores a goal. If the outplayed team go on to win the game, it will be described as a 'smash-and-grab victory'

Aggregate The combined score of matches between two teams in a two-legged tie

As good as a goal Used by commentators to describe an incredible save by a keeper, a goal-line clearance by a defender or a last-ditch block or sliding tackle

Assist A pass that directly leads to a goal being scored

Away-goals rule If a two-legged cup tie finishes level on aggregate, the winner is determined by the team that scored the most goals away from home. This is currently used in the Champions League and the Europa League, but not in English cup comps

B

Big-game player Someone who always performs on the big stage in a high-pressure situation, such as a cup final or an important league match. These big-game players are not bothered by nerves or overwhelmed by the occasion and will often produce a moment of magic to win a game

Brace A term used when a player scores two goals in a match

Bust-up Normally used to describe a heated incident between two team-mates, which generally erupts during a training session

C

Cap What a player is said to receive when he or she plays for their country. One appearance for the national team, equals one international cap

Catenaccio An Italian term for a very defensive tactical formation and style of play. The word means 'door bolt' and was used famously by the successful Inter Milan team of the 1960s

Clean sheet When a team successfully stops the opposition from scoring a goal, they are said to have kept a clean sheet. Keepers absolutely love these

Consolation goal When a losing team scores a goal late on in a game that has no impact on the final result

Cup-tied When a player is not allowed to play in a cup competition because they have already played in the same comp for a different club in an earlier round

D

David and Goliath A biblical story about Goliath, a giant, who was defeated in battle by a young man called David. Subsequently used by football pundits to describe a match between a big club and a much smaller side

Dead-ball specialist A player who is particularly good at taking set-pieces, specifically free-kicks and corners

Derby A match between two, usually local, teams with a long-standing rivalry. Also a Championship club

Diamond A formation that doesn't use wingers or wide players. It consists of four midfielders – one holding midfielder playing deep, one attacking midfielder behind the strikers and two central midfielders, one playing to the left and one playing to the right. On paper it looks like a diamond shape, hence the name

Dissent When a player uses offensive language or makes an offensive gesture towards the officials – this will normally result in a yellow or red card being brandished

TERMS 100 definitions of things you'll hear in footy!

Double Most commonly used when a club wins both its domestic league and its country's major cup competition in the same season

Downing tools A player who's not happy with their team-mates or manager will sometimes 'down tools' – meaning they will put zero effort in during matches and training sessions

E

Early bath Another term for being sent off or shown a red card. When a player is dismissed, they will be the first one back in the changing room and, traditionally, the first one to hop into the big communal bath

Engine A player with good stamina is said to have a good engine. Only ever refers to midfielders and wing-backs

Extra-time An additional period of two 15-minute halves of football, used to determine the winner in some cup matches that finish all-square after 90 minutes. This is often when a manager will throw on some fresh legs

F

False nine Traditionally, a team's central striker would wear the No.9 shirt, but when operating as a false nine a team's central forward is given licence to roam. When the false nine drops into the hole, it creates problems for the opposition centre-backs who either follow the player and leave space in behind for the other attackers to exploit, or they allow the false nine time and space on the ball and get punished for it. Lionel Messi perfected this role in Pep Guardiola's Barcelona team from 2009 to 2012

Fever When a lower-league team reaches the third round of the FA Cup or beyond, their town is said to have cup fever. Local shops, especially butchers, often show their support for their town's football teams with colourful displays in their windows

Fortress The name given to the stadium of a team that has a brilliant home record. For example: 'During the 2020-21 season, Fulham won just two home games – Craven Cottage was NOT a fortress'

G

Gaffer A less formal name for the manager, boss or head coach

Galactico A high-profile, global superstar who moves for a huge transfer fee. The term became popular in the early 2000s, thanks to Real Madrid's transfer policy of signing expensive, world-famous players, such as Zinedine Zidane, Ronaldo and David Beckham, who were then referred to as Galacticos

Genuine pace Used when talking about a very fast player. Not a moderately fast player, but a player with searing, blistering, lightning, explosive, genuine pace

Giant-killing When a team is beaten by a much smaller club in a cup competition – specifically a Premier League club by a lower-league or non-league team. See also 'David and Goliath' and 'Underdog'

Glory hunter A 'fan' who swaps clubs to follow the most successful team at the time

GOAT A version of G.O.A.T, which stands for 'Greatest of all time'

Group of Death A group in a tournament (such as the World Cup or Euros) that is made up entirely of very strong teams

H

Hat-trick When one player scores three goals in a single game. A perfect hat-trick is when the goals come from the left foot, the right foot and the head

Holding role A midfield position where the main job is to protect the defence by tackling and breaking up play before starting counter-attacks

Hospital pass A careless pass that puts the receiver at risk of being injured or places them in instant danger of being dispossessed

Howler A huge mistake. Most commonly committed by keepers conceding silly goals or by bumbling centre-backs scoring own goals

I

In his pocket When a defensive player has kept an attacking opponent quiet for the whole game, it is said that he's had him 'in his pocket'

Injury time The time added on by a referee at the end of 90 minutes, based on the number of stoppages (for example, injuries, substitutions, goals) during the game. Also known as added time or stoppage time

In the hole The space on the pitch between the midfield and the attack, normally inhabited by No.10s and false nines

J

Journeyman A footballer who has played for many clubs during their career. To qualify as a genuine journeyman, a player should list at least 12 clubs on their Wikipedia profile. The opposite of a one-club man

K

Kill the game A goal that is usually scored in the final minutes of a match and gives the scoring team some breathing space over their opponents

Knock A small injury

Knuckleball A method of kicking the ball so that it produces almost no spinning motion during its flight. This type of shot, made famous by Cristiano Ronaldo, is usually used for long-range shots or free-kicks

L

Limbs A term used to describe a large group of fans wildly celebrating a goal scored by their team

Lost the dressing room When a manager no longer has influence and control over their players, and is rewarded by poor, uninterested displays by these players on matchday

Lottery Used by some to describe a team's chance of winning a penalty shootout

M

Managerial merry-go-round What failed managers are said to be on as soon as they are sacked – they are just waiting on the merry-go-round until another club is persuaded to give them a job

Man-to-man marking A system of marking where each player is responsible for an opposing player, rather than an area of the pitch. This normally refers to defending set-pieces, but sometimes managers will ask their best defender to go man to man on the opposition team's danger man. Compare with zonal marking

Mickey Mouse cup A cup competition considered to be of a low standard and of very little importance

Mixer The penalty area when crowded with players. A team, especially one chasing a late equaliser or winner, will be encouraged to get the ball into the mixer

N

No-nonsense Can describe a big, tough-tackling defender or the type of clearance this defender will regularly make

No-man's land Where a keeper finds himself after having a rush of blood to the head and racing from his goal-line but is then stranded, with no chance of getting to the ball and having left his goal unattended

TERMS
100 definitions of things you'll hear in footy!

Nutmeg A football skill whereby the ball is put through the legs of another player. Also known as a panna

O

One-club man A player who spends their entire career with one club. Ryan Giggs (Man. United), Paolo Maldini (AC Milan) and Francesco Totti (Roma) are examples

One for the cameras The description of a relatively routine save made to look more complicated and spectacular than necessary by a keeper

P

Panenka A type of penalty that is chipped delicately down the middle of the goal after the keeper has already dived, expecting a firmly struck shot into the corner. Named after the Czech footballer Antonin Panenka, who introduced it at the European Championship in 1976

Panic buy To make a last-minute signing, normally on transfer-deadline day, of a player that your team neither wants or needs

Park the bus An often-criticised tactic that means to play very defensively, to sit back, get a lot of players behind the ball and to offer no attacking threat. Effectively, it's the same as simply parking a bus in front of your goal

Playmaker A talented attacking player whose job is to control the tempo of their team's play. Regularly praised for their passing and vision

Pomp When a player or a team were at their peak or enjoying some relative success, they are said to have been in their pomp

Pressing When the team without the ball put lots of pressure on the team in possession. By frantically chasing and harassing the players in possession, the aim is to win the ball back as close to the opposition's goal as possible by tackling them or forcing them into errors

Q

Quarterback A deep-lying playmaker who sprays passes around. Taken from the similar position in American football

R

Rabona The technique of kicking the ball, where the kicking leg is crossed behind the back of the standing leg. Incidentally, 'rabona' is the Spanish word for skipping school

S

Schoolboy A way of describing any defensive error that is the result of inexperience

Sitter When a player misses an incredibly easy goalscoring opportunity – often when the ball has been laid on a plate for them

Six-pointer A crunch match between two teams who are both competing for the title, promotion or for survival. The difference between winning and losing can result in a six-point gap in the table

Skipper Another name for the captain. Often shortened to skip

THE A-Z OF KEY FOOTBALL

Slammed A way of responding angrily to something. A manager can slam a rival for club for tapping up one of his players, while the football world slammed the big six's plan to form a breakaway European Super League. Alternatives to slammed are 'blasted', 'hit out at' and 'lambasted'

Slammed home Can refer to a well-hit penalty that is said to be slammed home. Can also be used to describe a goal that has been scored after the keeper has made a save but not held onto it – the rebound being, sometimes emphatically, slammed home

Squad rotation A fairly new approach to team selection, whereby a manager will swap and change his starting line-up from one week to the next to keep his players fit and fresh over the course of a season

Squad player A player who isn't a first-team regular but will be called upon when a manager has an injury crisis, a tired squad or is picking a line-up for a Mickey Mouse cup match

Stepover A skill used when dribbling. This involves the dribbler moving their foot over the ball, without touching it, in order to confuse an opponent by making them think they're going to move in a direction they're not intending to. A big favourite of Cristiano Ronaldo

Sweeper The name given to a central defender whose job is to drop off and 'sweep up' trouble behind the other centre-backs. Sweepers needs to be good on the ball as they will be expected to start attacks by passing the ball or running out of defence into midfield with it

Sweeper keeper This type of keeper patrols the edge of their penalty area and is happy to race out of their box to clean up anything that comes within 30 yards of the penalty box. Germany's Manuel Neuer is the most-famous example of a sweeper keeper

T

Tapping up When a club tries to convince a player, who is contracted to another club, to sign for them without asking his current club for permission to do so

Target man A specific type of striker, who is strong, good in the air and often used to hold up the ball or lay off passes to their team-mates

Tifo A colourful, coordinated display by supporters using flags, signs or banners inside a stadium

Tekkers Short for the word technique, but also used when describing a sick piece of skill

Tiki-taka A style of football that involves dominating possession and passing the ball quickly in order to create space and pull the opposition players out of position as they chase the ball. It is associated with Pep Guardiola's Barcelona team of 2008-2012 and the all-conquering Spain team that won Euro 2008, World Cup 2010 and Euro 2012

Top bins The top corner of a goal. Used specifically when a player scores by kicking the ball into that part of the goal

Total football A style of football that was invented by Ajax and the Holland teams of the 1970s. The idea is that any player on the team can play in any position at any time, allowing a free-flowing, fluid, dynamic approach

Transfer window The period during the season in which a football club can spend huge amounts to bring in some shiny new players and get shot of the ones they no longer want

TERMS
100 definitions of things you'll hear in footy!

Treble When a club wins its domestic league, its country's major cup and the Champions League in the same season. Sometimes also used, wrongly, when a team wins any three trophies in the same campaign

Trequartista An Italian word that translates as 'three-quarters' and describes a playmaker who operates behind the striker but in front of the midfield. Also known as a No.10

Trialist A player who plays for a club on a trial basis, often in the hope of being offered a full-time contract

U

Underdog A team not expected to win a particular game or competition because they are much smaller, and considered weaker, than the opposition

Up-and-over What a dead-ball specialist needs to do when taking a direct free-kick just outside the penalty area. He needs to get the ball up and over the wall, but also needs it to dip in time, so it doesn't go sailing over the crossbar

Up-and-under A lobbed pass or clearance that has normally been hoofed forward without any great level of skill or finesse

Utility player A player who is able to play in a number of different positions – a good squad player to have

V

VAR An abbreviation of video assistant referee – a match official who reviews decisions made by the on-pitch referee with the use of video footage and a headset for communication

Volley A shot, or sometimes a pass, in which the ball is kicked before it touches the ground

W

Window Can be used when talking about the transfer window (see p160) but also where a team's form goes out of when they play in a local derby

Worldy A term for a goal that is considered to be world-class. Worldies are normally long-range efforts, bicycle kicks or thumping volleys

X

xG An abbreviation for expected goals – a relatively new statistical measurement, which analyses the quality of chances created by a team and the likelihood of them being scored. For example, a shot from two yards out has a much higher xG rating than a shot from the halfway line

Y

Yo-yo club A team that regularly bounces between divisions – most commonly used when referring to promotion to and relegation from the Premier League

Z

Zonal marking A system of marking in which each player is responsible for an area of the pitch – or an area of the penalty box when defending set-pieces. The opposite of man-to-man marking